THE PSYCHOLOGY
OF INTELLIGENCE

What fascinates us about intelligence? How does intelligence impact our daily lives? Why do we sometimes fear intelligence?

Human intelligence is a vital resource, yet the study of it is pervaded by neglect and misconceptions. *The Psychology of Intelligence* helps make sense of the contradictory social attitudes and practices in relation to intelligence that we have seen over the decades, from the idea that it drove eugenicist policies and actions in the past, to our current backlash against "experts" and critical thinking. Showing how our approach to intelligence impacts our everyday lives in educational, occupational, medical, and legal settings, the book asks if it is possible to lift the taboo and move beyond the prejudices surrounding intelligence.

Challenging popular assumptions, *The Psychology of Intelligence* encourages us to face intelligence in ourselves and others as an important fact of life that we can all benefit from embracing more openly.

Sonja Falck is a Senior Lecturer at the University of East London, UK, and a UKCP and BACP accredited psychotherapist and supervisor. She consults in person and online internationally, specialising in high-ability adults' relationship issues.

THE PSYCHOLOGY OF EVERYTHING

People are fascinated by psychology, and what makes humans tick. Why do we think and behave the way we do? We've all met armchair psychologists claiming to have the answers, and people that ask if psychologists can tell what they're thinking. *The Psychology of Everything* is a series of books which debunk the popular myths and pseudo-science surrounding some of life's biggest questions.

The series explores the hidden psychological factors that drive us, from our subconscious desires and aversions, to our natural social instincts. Absorbing, informative, and always intriguing, each book is written by an expert in the field, examining how research-based knowledge compares with popular wisdom, and showing how psychology can truly enrich our understanding of modern life.

Applying a psychological lens to an array of topics and contemporary concerns – from sex, to fashion, to conspiracy theories – *The Psychology of Everything* will make you look at everything in a new way.

Titles in the series:

For further information about this series please visit www.routledge textbooks.com/textbooks/thepsychologyofeverything/

THE PSYCHOLOGY OF INTELLIGENCE

SONJA FALCK

Routledge
Taylor & Francis Group

LONDON AND NEW YORK

First published 2021
by Routledge
2 Park Square, Milton Park, Abingdon, Oxon OX14 4RN

and by Routledge
52 Vanderbilt Avenue, New York, NY 10017

Routledge is an imprint of the Taylor & Francis Group, an informa business

British Library Cataloguing-in-Publication Data
A catalogue record for this book is available from the British Library

Library of Congress Cataloging-in-Publication Data
A catalog record for this book has been requested

ISBN: 978-0-367-48707-2 (hbk)
ISBN: 978-0-367-48293-0 (pbk)
ISBN: 978-1-003-04236-5 (ebk)

Typeset in Joanna
by Apex CoVantage, LLC

Printed and bound by CPI Group (UK) Ltd, Croydon, CR0 4YY

CONTENTS

ILLUSTRATIONS

TABLES

FIGURES

ACKNOWLEDGEMENTS

I am grateful to all of my family, friends, colleagues, and clients who have in their many different ways contributed to and supported my writing of this book. My thanks specifically for contributions made by Dr Rachael Klug; Harry Eyres; Judith Balcazar; Anthony Harvison; Andrew and Sheridan; Maya Dominique Fay-Carlyle; Prof John Radford; and Rebecca Howell, Senior Education Consultant for Potential Plus UK. Thank you to Damon Falck for his incisive comments in spite of huge disruptions during the coronavirus/COVID-19 crisis.

I thank my editors at Routledge – April Peake, who suggested the project to me and sped it from inception through to contract in record time, and Alex Howard, who responsively saw it through to conclusion. My deep appreciation to Max Eames for his reliably efficient, humorous, and insightful critiquing of the draft manuscript.

My very special thanks to Richard Harding for his generosity and considerable sacrifices in making a brilliant writing retreat possible for me, and to Lawrence Falck, who has shown such admirable forbearance in his enduring of my periods of intense concentration necessary to complete the book.

EXPLAINING THE BOOK
A new way of viewing
human intelligence

I love intelligence. As a phenomenon, and as a subject. And yet I hate telling people that intelligence is one of the main themes in my work, because it always attracts complicated reactions. This week a psychotherapist whose work I supervise suddenly said to me, "What is it like for you to work with me?" I was surprised at the question. I asked why she was asking me that. Next thing, she was in tears. "Because you work so much with intelligence", she said. "I'm worried that I am disappointing for you". I hope this book will demonstrate why it is completely understandable that this supervisee of mine could have had that worry, and also demonstrate that the perspectives I hold mean that she had nothing to worry about. I hope this book will help people to tackle the way of viewing intelligence that leads to that worry.

This book is firmly focused on human intelligence rather than artificial intelligence. It is currently very fashionable to be interested in machine-based intelligence and very unfashionable to draw attention to human intelligence. I see human intelligence as a vital resource worthy of being paid attention.

Within the field of psychology there is no subject that has been more intensively studied than the subject of human intelligence, and none that has been more contentious. In addressing this subject, this book has a different purpose from that of other books you will find on human intelligence. Such books tend to set about examining intelligence as a trait that can be approached objectively, and they systematically scrutinise it in the following ways: theoretically (making models of what intelligence is and how it works); psychometrically (measuring intelligence with psychological tests); genetically (studying which parts of our DNA relate to intelligence); and neuroscientifically (finding out how intelligence is impacted by the anatomy and workings of our brains).

By contrast, this book examines our subjectivity in relation to intelligence. This means that it examines our personal psychological and social responses to intelligence. As put by one of the five experts in the field of intelligence who reviewed my proposal for this book, the book's focus is on "the human-side" of intelligence, which is often overlooked. This means that – while the book will say something about each of the dimensions listed in the previous paragraph – and also provide many endnote references for where you can read more about them – its main focus is to explore intelligence as something that we all have reactions to, have attitudes and feelings towards, and make interpretations about, not just on our own but in relation to one other.

I also aim to show how it is the interpersonal psychology of how we feel about each other and relate to each other that underlies the way that intelligence as a phenomenon is, and has been, dealt with in Western society. Over the decades we have seen the unfolding of powerfully emotive and conflicting reactions to the prominent and important subject of intelligence. Using the psychosocial (psychological and social) emphasis I have described this book will provide a way of viewing intelligence that makes sense of its contradictory history and the associated opposing policies and practices in relation to intelligence that we have seen over the decades.

WHAT WILL READING THIS BOOK DO FOR YOU?

As you read this sentence, you are reading at a particular point in time, and at this point in time the social attitudes, cultural practices, and teachings about intelligence are the way that they are because of what has played out in the past. Even the way that the currently most popular psychology textbooks present the topic of intelligence – which has been shown to often be inaccurate[1] – is influenced by this. Without knowing this, you could read such a textbook and not have a sense of why certain content is being included rather than other content or realise which biases might be present. You could be unaware of how the selection of information that you are being exposed to is likely to shape your beliefs about and attitudes towards the subject and perhaps even leave you with false impressions about it.

The current book invites you to take a step back and think about the historical and psychosocial context within which you are reading right now. By gaining an understanding of this you will gain a framework which can be used – if you wish to use it – to contextualise and evaluate any other book or article that you read on intelligence. You can also use it to evaluate the approaches that you see people around you taking towards intelligence. And you can use it to evaluate your own approach to intelligence.

The framework I am offering involves dividing the last approximately 200 years of the subject of intelligence in the Western world into three main ages. I view each of these three ages as having a distinct philosophical character and a distinct psychological character, and as involving a corresponding social change. Sociologists define social change as a significant alteration over time in behaviour patterns and cultural values and norms that yield profound social consequences, having long-term effects.

THREE AGES PHILOSOPHICALLY: THESIS, ANTITHESIS, SYNTHESIS

Eighteenth-century German philosopher Johann Fichte explained that the development of knowledge about a subject typically progresses in a pattern involving three sequential phases.[2] In the first phase, something is put forward as an attempted, or accepted, proposition, a formulating of a "thesis". After this, opposition to the thesis develops – the "antithesis". In this second phase, new ideas emerge that contradict and negate the thesis. In the third phase, an overview is developed of the content of both the thesis and the antithesis, resolving the conflict between their contradictory positions and bringing them together into a new integrated perspective, the "synthesis".

Each changing of phase constitutes what 20th-century American philosopher Thomas Kuhn called a "paradigm shift".[3] A paradigm is a prevailing structure of understanding and agreed reference points. With a paradigm shift the previously accepted paradigm is challenged and changes, bringing in a new structure of understanding and newly agreed reference points.

This book will explain the way Western society has engaged with the phenomenon of intelligence as unfolding over three ages that match, in sequence, this pattern of thesis, then antithesis, then synthesis. I will explain the first age, the thesis phase, as being pre–World War Two, and the second age, or antithesis phase, as following World War Two. And I will argue that we have been entering a third age since around 2015, in which we can reach a synthesis.

THREE AGES PSYCHOLOGICALLY: IDEALISATION, DEVALUATION, INTEGRATION

I will show that the previously described three phases also correspond to a psychological pattern that frequently plays out when we get involved with something – or someone – new. The first phase is idealisation. This is when you see only the good qualities in a new subject such as intelligence, or in your new job, or new lover, or the place you have moved to, seeing that as the best, putting it on a pedestal, seeing everything else as being by contrast unimportant.

In the next phase, what has been idealised comes to be devalued. Negative aspects begin to be noticed. Bad qualities. Suddenly what you were becoming involved with is no longer seen as perfect, and you feel disappointed, disillusioned, despondent. In devaluing it, you push it aside, embarrassed that you ever thought it was so wonderful. If, through this phase of devaluation, you don't actually abandon what you were becoming involved with, then relating to it in a different kind of way starts to develop.

Staying involved with something, or someone, beyond the early idealisation phase, and beyond the subsequent devaluation phase, can allow the nature of your involvement to develop a greater maturity. Instead of the more primitive way of functioning which splits the good (the idealised qualities) from the bad (the devalued qualities), a more mature way of functioning resolves these splits, making it possible for idealisation and devaluation to evolve into integration. Now something can come to be seen, and accepted, with all of its qualities – good and bad – as an integrated whole. For the first time, there can be an embracing of the full reality in all of its greater complexity.

The previous section outlined three ages in how Western society has engaged with the phenomenon of intelligence – the thesis phase, the antithesis phase, and the synthesis phase. I see the thesis phase as having involved an idealisation of intelligence, followed by the antithesis phase which involved a devaluation of intelligence. And I consider that we have started entering the synthesis phase, which is a psychological maturation and integration of the first two phases. The synthesis or integration offers a resolution of the tension and conflict that exist between those first two phases. I will explain this resolution as constituting an integrating of neurodiversity. (Neurodiversity means the diverse ways in which our brains can be different from each other in structure and function.) Throughout the book I will therefore refer to the three ages in Western society's approach to human intelligence as being the Age of Idealisation (the thesis phase, pre–World War Two); the Age of Devaluation (the antithesis phase, post–World War Two); and the Age of Integration (the synthesis phase, from about 2015 onwards).

THE BOOK'S SIMPLIFYING CONCEPTUAL FRAMEWORK

Table 0.1 gives a clear summary of this framework of three ages that this book is offering. The subsequent chapters will fully explain all the columns of the table. I will throughout refer to evidence from publications, research, and social phenomena to support this conceptualisation and to argue for why I am defining the time periods in the way that I am.

It is important to note, however, that with any change in age, there are forerunners in thought before a new social change gathers momentum, as well as – after a new social change has gathered momentum – holdovers of previous eras' policies and practices that can take many years to be fully concluded and replaced with new ones. For this reason, any identifying of main themes or progressions in a long and complicated series of historical events inevitably constitutes a simplification. But in putting forward such a simplifying conceptual framework, I am offering what is hopefully a useful way of thinking about and making sense of the major shifts in the field of intelligence that have been visible to date. I am doing so in the spirit of wanting to enable readers to clearly track my own thinking through this contentious field as well as inviting you to bring to it your own thinking and observations and join in the conversation.

Table 0.1 The book's framework: three ages in Western society's approach to human intelligence

Three ages psychologically	Approximate time periods involved	Position regarding nature versus nurture	Corresponding significant social changes	Three ages philosophically
Age of Idealisation	Pre–World War Two	Nature overruling nurture	Culminating in eugenics	The thesis phase
Age of Devaluation	Post–World War Two	Nurture overruling nature	Culminating in expertise	The antithesis phase
Age of Integration	The future: around 2015 onwards	Synthesis between nature and nurture	Integrating of neurodiversity	The synthesis phase

DEFINING INTELLIGENCE AND PSYCHOLOGY

There are numerous different definitions of what intelligence is and debates about what kinds of intelligence there might be. There will be representation of these different perspectives in the coming pages. However, to provide clarity of meaning, throughout this book my use of the word intelligence refers – unless stated otherwise – to general cognitive ability, also known as *g*, as discovered and defined by Charles Spearman in 1904.[4] This accords with the view of "mainstream science" on what intelligence is, as put forward in 1997 in an editorial with 52 signatories that appeared in the journal *Intelligence*. This defined general intelligence as "the ability to reason, plan, solve problems, think abstractly, comprehend complex ideas, learn quickly, and learn from experience".[5] The best measure we currently have of human intelligence is that of standardised IQ tests which yield a score in IQ points. The measuring of IQ will be critically explained in Chapter 2, and in that chapter and the next two there are specific headings related to the theorising and measuring of intelligence.

Psychology is defined as "the scientific study of how the mind works and how it influences behaviour".[6] How the mind works can involve brain physiology (anatomical structure and functioning) as well as the contents and patterns of our thoughts and the factors that influence these. As I am a practicing psychotherapist and a lecturer in counselling and psychotherapy, my psychological interest and expertise – that is, my interest and expertise in how the mind works and how it influences behaviour – lie less in brain physiology and more in the contents and patterns of our thoughts and the factors that influence these. Some of the factors that influence these are interpersonal bonds and interactions, social experiences, emotions, education (what we are taught), how we interpret things, motivations, culture, and beliefs. This psychosocial emphasis of mine, with a particularly relational approach – meaning a focus on how people relate to each other and are affected by those relations – will therefore be apparent in the way that I address the subject of intelligence.

My clients and students (and friends) are multinational and multicultural, and I have travelled widely around the world. However, as I grew up in South Africa and have lived in London, UK, for most of my adult life, my perspective is most shaped by my experiences of those two countries. Being based in the UK means that I will inevitably write more about how things are in the UK than elsewhere. There has been a lot of work around the subject of intelligence in the USA, and that will also be reflected.

THE IMPORTANCE OF INTELLIGENCE

This book also aims to convey how important the subject of intelligence is. It will present evidence of how intelligence has been strongly correlated with multiple different outcomes in life. I will show how in the Age of Idealisation intelligence came to be seen as indeed being of major importance, but that the way this was dealt with developed in such an alarming manner that in the Age of Devaluation there was a reaction of wanting to banish it, creating a backlash against perceiving intelligence as being of any importance at all.

I will argue that in the Age of Integration accurate information about intelligence could helpfully be incorporated into many areas of education so that its importance is no longer negated nor ignored, but that it should also definitely be dealt with differently than in the past. In this way a realistic but more balanced and humane and progressive path forward can be forged for the future. Other authors[7] have also called for the necessity of promoting better education around the subject of intelligence, and my intent is that this book will contribute towards that objective.

STRUCTURE OF THE BOOK

After the present short introduction, Chapter 1 concentrates on how we use intelligence in our daily lives, how we feel about it, and how intelligence makes us feel about ourselves and each other. The next three chapters (Chapters 2, 3, and 4) are devoted, one each, to explaining the previously outlined three ages in Western society's way of engaging with the phenomenon of intelligence. Each chapter will visit certain core issues – the measuring of intelligence, theories of intelligence, researching intelligence, intelligence-related discrimination, and the underlying psychology – to show how these core issues differ across the different ages. Chapter 5 presents and discusses how human intelligence is applied in various contemporary settings – educational, occupational, medical, and legal – showing how the three ages relate to these. The book ends with a short concluding chapter that consolidates this way of making sense of the history and current status of the subject of human intelligence. It emphasises that if we want to make a change in our approach to intelligence, we first need to understand and tackle the underlying psychology. You are invited to choose the approach that you wish to take towards intelligence: I encourage readers to see intelligence as a fact of life that it would be of benefit to all of us to face and more openly embrace.

1

INTELLIGENCE IN OUR DAILY LIVES

It was time for the weekly session of one of my regular clients, Ida (for confidentiality that's not her real name). Ida walked into my consulting room looking like she was preparing herself to raise something difficult with me. She lay down on the couch, took a deep breath, and said: "There's something I've been avoiding with you. I am avoiding intelligence. And I've bought your book *Extreme Intelligence*, but I'm avoiding reading it. Because I realise I am afraid of intelligence". She went on to tell me a heart-breaking story of an experience she had as a child that has ever since determined the way she feels about her own intelligence and intelligence in others, as well as how she reacts to – or avoids – the subject.

Ida had a chaotic upbringing and suffered serious neglect in a home where there was alcoholism and abuse. No-one was paying any attention to what a struggle it was for her to survive. Unable to hold it all together, she often ran away from school. However, there was one subject – biology – that she lived for. She loved it and would get absolutely absorbed in reading about it. One day the biology teacher pulled her aside and said to her "I don't know why you're spending all this time doing all that reading. There's no point, because all you're ever going to be is a social dropout".

In Ida's school, as is typical, academic interest and achievement were associated with intelligence. She admired this teacher's mastery of his subject as a sign of his intelligence, but experienced him as using it against her, to reject her. His declaration of academic involvement as something irrelevant for her left her feeling that intelligence was something possessed by and recognised in others, but absent in herself, and that others' intelligence was something she could be hurt by.

I have started with Ida's story as an example of how feeling positively or negatively about intelligence comes to be shaped, beginning in our childhoods. Each of us, if we take a moment to think about it, has a story of our own about how experiences we had while growing up have affected our views and attitudes towards intelligence. Our experiences could have left us feeling that we are overall pretty stupid, or overall pretty smart. That self-concept then moulds our assumptions about how others see us and what they expect of us, as well as what we expect we are ourselves capable of.[1] This in turn impacts how we behave, affecting what tasks we take on or avoid. This chapter focuses on how we feel about intelligence, how intelligence makes us feel about ourselves and each other, and how intelligence manifests in our daily lives. It also begins to explore what might constitute "stupid" or "smart".

INTELLIGENCE EVERYWHERE

Intelligence is a subject that affects every single one of us. We will examine over the course of this book how ideas, prejudices, and assumptions about intelligence underlie the way our educational systems are constructed, the way our businesses are conducted, and the way we treat each other. If we are impressed by something someone does, we often call it intelligent. Negative violations of behaviour expectations – in other words, someone doing something we don't like – we call stupid.[2] And we are always assessing – often unconsciously, and often instantaneously – what we consider the level of intelligence to be of the people we encounter.

We are actually quite good at such assessments. Research has shown that there is a significant correlation – and much higher than by chance – between people's measured intelligence and what others perceive their level of intelligence to be based on what their faces look like[3] and how they behave, including language use[4] and nonverbal behaviour.[5] For example, the stable facial features that are associated with intelligence include face height, interpupillary distance, and nose size: taller faces, wider-set eyes, and larger noses are perceived as more intelligent.[6] Transitory facial cues – meaning those that can be affected by, for example, tiredness – that are associated with intelligence include eyelid openness and mouth curvature: more open eyes and slightly upturned corners of the mouth are perceived as more intelligent.[7]

In terms of behaviour, people are perceived as being more intelligent the more upright their body posture is, the more responsive they are to a conversational partner, the more they hold eye gaze while they are listening to someone and while they are speaking, the clearer and faster their speech is, and the more they use hand gestures while talking.[8] Fidgeting prompts others to form a lower estimation of your intelligence.[9] In summary it is behaviours that are engaged, attentive, and watchful that are perceived as intelligent.

These kinds of evaluations that we all make have a considerable impact in social situations. Seeking similarity in intelligence is a significant element involved in how we choose friends and lovers: research has confirmed that regardless of sex, race, and other variables, children create best-friend pairs by bonding with peers who are strongly correlated in intelligence.[10] This has also been shown to be true of romantic partners, where people choose mates based more on similarity in intelligence than in personality or physical traits.[11] Different sources have suggested that in personal and professional relationships there is a "zone of tolerance" between people of about 20 IQ points[12], and that a difference in IQ of greater than 30 points presents a prohibitive communication barrier.[13]

In recruitment settings, job interviewers make judgments about candidates' intelligence which can then bias their hiring decisions.[14] When we choose business leaders, we prefer individuals whom we see as being more intelligent.[15] In organisational contexts, respective levels of intelligence between leaders and followers influence whether a leader succeeds: it is that same discrepancy in IQ of greater than 30 points between a leader and his or her followers that has been shown to cause leadership failure.[16]

From these findings a key realisation emerges: intelligence is something that people are always noticing and looking out for in each other, even if they do not explicitly think about or talk about how they are doing this. From this it is also apparent that intelligence is treated as a trait that exists in individuals, and in varying levels in various individuals, and that the principle of compatibility is important: personal and professional relationships are more successful where levels of intelligence are matched between individuals. The successful carrying out of tasks is another area where a matching of intelligence is necessary – in this case, the matching of intelligence to the demands of the task.

USING INTELLIGENCE IN DAILY LIFE: MATCHING INTELLIGENCE TO TASK

The matching of intelligence to task might again be something that is often not consciously thought about, or not outside of formal selection procedures in educational or occupational contexts. But there are dozens of daily activities where different levels of intelligence are required and where people self-select to take on or avoid a task according to what they find a comfortable cognitive match. For example, in London, this is apparent in the options that are available in several supermarkets for how to conduct and pay for your shopping. (Although it must be remembered that what tasks any given person chooses to take on or avoid at any given time is not just about level of actual cognitive capability. This is affected by several other factors, including self-concept – as described previously – and motivation, as well as the energy a person has for exerting themselves. However, the next paragraphs refer to the use of everyday technologies, and research has shown that ease of use of everyday technologies is related to cognitive capability, with people who have cognitive impairments struggling to use such technologies.[17])

The traditional, and also the intellectually simplest, way of carrying out your shopping, is to fill your shopping basket then queue up at a check-out till that is operated by a cashier. You pass your items to that person, who logs them through the till. He or she then tells you how much to pay and takes your payment and processes it for you. Here you don't have to do any thinking for yourself, and you have someone else's help all the way through the task.

A relatively recent development, one which demands more cognitive exertion, is the alternative where you fill your basket and then take it to a self-check-out till. There you scan all the items yourself and also process the payment yourself. This method of payment requires being able to self-navigate the technology involved, initiate the steps needed, and complete them correctly in the correct sequence.

An even more recent development, which is the most intellectually demanding of all, is the option where, every time you take an item off the shelf, you use your own smart phone to scan the item *before* packing it into your basket. (Or, with this option you can pack the items directly into your shopping bag.) At the end of such a shop you have to use a different functionality at the self-check-out till, which involves scanning your phone against the machine and completing that transaction correctly together with the processing of the payment.

This last method has the advantages for shoppers of providing the greatest independence and vastly reducing the time spent at check-out tills. And it has the advantages to supermarkets of lowering costs by reducing the number of staff members and check-out tills that they need to supply. However, it is also the method that is least frequently used. In a general population it will always be the smallest number of people who will voluntarily choose to take on tasks that involve the highest level of independence and complexity, and this generally corresponds with distribution of intelligence within a population (see the bell curve explained in the next chapter). Greater intelligence is required in order to learn and master more complex tasks.

Given varying levels of intelligence within a society, there always has to be provision of different methods or routes for achieving basic necessary tasks such as the weekly undertaking of food shopping. There also have to be ways of identifying which individuals will be suitable for carrying out necessary societal functions of varying complexity. For example, one simple and low-risk – and essential – task is the weekly removal of garbage from households. One complex and high-risk task is the safe piloting of very high-expense, high-powered, and high-speed aircraft that have the responsibility for hundreds of lives, whether as commercial passenger jets or as war-time fighter planes. Finding some way of assessing intelligence therefore becomes a key element of formal selection procedures in educational and occupational settings that seek to make appropriate matches between cognitive capability and task. And the adept accomplishment of the most complex of tasks, together with the securing of positions in society that involve carrying out such tasks effectively, typically attracts fascination and prestige precisely because it is a minority of people who manage to achieve such feats.

OUR FASCINATION WITH INTELLIGENCE

Alcatraz is probably the most famous "super-maximum security"[18] prison ever designed. Opened as a federal penitentiary in 1934, it was situated on an island of impenetrable rock off the coast of San Francisco, USA, surrounded by swift and erratic frigid tides that make swimming practically impossible. The nearest shore point is one-and-a-half miles away. Now disused, the four cellblocks on the island housed 600 individual cells and each had 18-inch-thick reinforced concrete walls and steel fronts. A network of gun towers trained searchlights over the grounds. In nearly 30 years of operation very few had the hubris to even attempt escape.

Contrary to all of these odds, on the night of 11 June 1962 three inmates disappeared without ever being traced. A fourth convict – Allen West – was meant to be with them, but on the night of escape he encountered a problem that caused him to be left behind. After that he agreed to share the details of how their bid for freedom had been meticulously planned.

It had all been masterminded by Frank Morris, age 35, who had had a lifetime of crime related to robbery. The escape plan involved collaborating with his fellow inmates to inventively source materials for improvising the tools and equipment they needed, and persevering together secretively over a period of six months to make all the necessary preparations. They made lifelike dummy heads that tricked the patrolling guards into thinking they were asleep in their beds, tunnelled through the cement behind their cells, climbed the ventilation shaft to the top, drilled through the roof, kept within what they had identified as the watchtowers' blind spot, scaled two 12-foot barbed-wire fences, and then paddled away into the night on homemade flotation devices.

Succeeding at this supposedly impossible feat of escaping from Alcatraz – which has been called the greatest escape in American history – set Morris apart from ordinary people. Another – very related – way in which he was set apart is that he had an IQ score of 133,[19] meaning that his measured intelligence was higher than that of 98% of people. This score puts him in the range of what is classified as "giftedness", or what I prefer to call extreme intelligence or intellectual agility. His behaviour certainly has all the hallmarks of high intelligence, such as seeking to acquire new knowledge and skills, wilfulness, persistence, and creative adaptation of resources. High intelligence easily makes a riveting story: we are fascinated by intelligence precisely because of it being colloquially associated with – and scientifically correlated with – the highest of human achievement. Albert Einstein, Marie Curie, Leonardo da Vinci, Ludwig van Beethoven: geniuses like these are people we admire and are inspired by.

Research conducted over a period of more than 100 years has proven that intelligence is the variable that has the strongest impact on the largest number of life outcomes. These include mental and physical health and illness, life expectancy, educational attainment, income, job performance, criminal behaviour, dementia, and even death by motorcar accident.[20] Given that it is such a fundamental and influential trait, intelligence could be expected to be something that is widely and openly acknowledged and talked about. The fact that this is not the case reflects the complicated history and relationship we have with intelligence – collectively as a society but also, often, personally.

OUR FEAR OF INTELLIGENCE

My client Ida said that she realised she was avoiding intelligence because she was *afraid* of it. Why might intelligence be feared? In the research interviews I conducted with individuals whose IQ is in the top 2% of the population, several had experienced being described by others as "scarily intelligent". People feel most at ease when they are within their "comfort zone", which is a psychological state in which a person feels familiar with what is around them and perceives themselves to be in control of what may happen, therefore feeling secure and experiencing low levels of anxiety and stress. It appears to be the case that perceiving someone as being very intelligent creates an anticipation that he or she might say or do something that is outside of one's familiar range of expectation and understanding, which could take one by surprise, with a negative implication. A synonym for being intelligent is being "sharp": something that is sharp can hurt. When we realise that someone else has knowledge, skill, foresight, or a power of analysis that is beyond our own, we often greet it as threatening. Let's consider for a moment that this is something that you can remember – or imagine – yourself experiencing: what exactly is the nature of the threat that is involved?

One type of threat involved is a threat to your own sense of competence. Noticing someone else's greater competence can make you feel that in comparison with them, you are perhaps less equipped to master your environment than you had believed you were. That can make you feel less competent within yourself and consequently more vulnerable in relation to your environment. That does not feel good and therefore is not welcomed.

A second threat is that if someone uses their competence to point out something you didn't know or remember, or to show that there is a better way of doing something than the way you were doing it, you might feel exposed as lacking and be embarrassed. This can make you feel judged by that person (and any witnesses) as being inadequate, as though that person is better than you, or you are worse than him or her. Again, that does not feel good. It could also have a more lasting effect of changing your status in others' eyes, and your own, not only by placing you as being inferior to the more competent person but also by lowering your status in comparison with the status you held previously.

A third threat is that noticing someone else's greater competence will make you realise that if there were to arise a conflict or competition between you, you would most likely be the loser. The possibility of losing to a smarter adversary is raised to epic scale in major stories in fiction and history that involve a compelling battle of good against evil, and in which there is always a high intelligence on either side being pitted against each other. For example, the legendary intelligence of fictional detective Sherlock Holmes enables him to outwit nearly everyone he meets in the course of the numerous cases he solves. However, the one person who is formidably matched with him in intelligence is his arch-enemy Moriarty. In another immensely popular story, young wizard Harry Potter fights for his life by using (with the help of his friends) superior intellectual reasoning (and some magic) to understand, locate, and destroy the horcruxes which are diabolical Voldemort's ingenious insurances against mortality. In cinematic saga *Star Wars*, "the Force" is accessible to Luke Skywalker and the Jedi Knights, who wield it for good. But it is also accessible to Darth Vader and the Sith, who put it to malevolent use. An example in history is that of World War Two, which saw several nations grouping together to gather intelligence that could overthrow the malign genius of Hitler and his allies. Even in religion, the omniscience and omnipotence of God meets sophisticated challenge from the similarly powerful but evil Lucifer. Characters like Voldemort, Darth Vader, Hitler, and Satan encapsulate sinister intelligences that we fear.

From all of this it makes sense that when we shy away from intelligence we can be seeking to avoid feeling bad about ourselves, or seeking to avoid losing out to a potential rival or enemy. There are clearly good reasons to fear intelligence given the threats it can present connected with competence, status, competition, and even survival. However, what has been described so far relates to how we might be affected when encountering impressive intelligence in others. How do we respond when we encounter in others what appears to be a deficit in intelligence?

RESPONDING TO THE VARIABILITY AND RELATIVITY OF INTELLIGENCE

A first principle to remember in appraising levels of intelligence is that intelligence is relative. Until and unless we have learned the importance of mediating our expectations, we automatically expect others to function at a similar cognitive level to our own. An example of this is that in my research, my very high-IQ interviewees would typically confuse ability with motivation. This means that they would see a person's failure to achieve something that they themselves could achieve as being because that person was lazy (unmotivated), rather than realising that that person – unlike themselves – did not have the ability to achieve in the same way.

We also adapt to the general level of intelligence that we are used to experiencing around us. It is common that a student who is out-performing everyone else in a small, mixed-ability school (the "big fish in a small pond" phenomenon) will be treated as – and experience themselves as – highly intellectually capable. If such a student then moves to a large selective university where he or she is for the first time surrounded by others of equal or superior ability, no longer being academically the best often triggers a crisis of confidence and identity.

What we assume is intelligent behaviour can also vary according to culture. Most countries around the world associate intelligence with strong cognitive functioning, as evidenced in, for example, problem-solving performance. However, conceptions of intelligence are to some extent based on competence at activities that are cul-turally valued. And there are also some strikingly different emphases in what is considered intelligent in different countries. For example, something that is cited as a sign of intelligence in the USA is speedy thought,[21] which is specifically about cognitive performance. More of a focus on social behaviour is evident in Mali and Kenya, where listening to all aspects of an issue is cited as a sign of intelligence.[22] In India, modesty is cited,[23] and in China, benevolence and doing what is right.[24] These differences can relate to whether intelligence is seen as something principally cognitive (more typical in Western individualist cultures) or as something principally social (more typical in Eastern collectivist cultures).

We can also fail to recognise that a behaviour is intelligent if we cannot fathom it. Throughout history there have been repeated cases in which pioneering thinkers are ignored or vilified for work that only comes to be understood and valued after their deaths. One example is Italian astronomer, physicist, and engineer Galileo Galilei, who was convicted of heresy and placed under house arrest for the rest of his life for championing heliocentrism (the idea – now universally accepted – that the earth revolves around the sun).[25]

We might also fail to realise that a person's true intelligence is being masked by other issues. For example, my client Ida's poor performance at school had nothing to do with her level of intelligence and everything to do with her deprived circumstances. In later life, when she had recovered from her childhood trauma and was living in transformed circumstances, she demonstrated a capacity for advanced intellectual functioning and was able to enjoy associated achievements. If you used as an assessment of someone's intelligence the marker mentioned previously of holding eye gaze during conversation, you would be wrong if your conversational partner was autistic. Autistic people find it very hard to maintain eye contact but could be extremely intelligent: it has been found that there are higher rates of autism in people with very high IQ.[26] It is worth remembering that it is always possible for there to be other reasons at play than those which we think of at first. We might see an elderly gentleman queuing at a cashier-operated till in the supermarket and assume that he lacks the cognitive flexibility to learn the new self-check-out technologies, when actually what is motivating his behaviour is loneliness and the wish for a few moments of attention and friendly conversation from the cashier while she scans his shopping.

I am making these points towards recommending caution in making judgments about what another's level of intelligence is. However, having said all of that, there are situations in which it becomes obvious that a person has deficits in the ordinarily expected level of general human intelligence. An IQ score of 70 or lower would put a person in the range of what is classified as learning disability/ intellectual disability, and such a person would permanently need to have support with navigating daily life activities that people with average intelligence completely take for granted. Low IQ has been associated with challenging behaviour, dropping out of school, unemployment, poverty, frequency of injury, high rates of divorce, lower rates of marriage, higher rates of illegitimate births, welfare dependency, low citizenship involvement (caring least about political issues and voting least), and higher risk of criminal behaviour.[27]

Given the principle of compatibility in intelligence described previously, whenever two individuals try to communicate with each other who have a large gap between them in intellectual ability, a sense of difficulty and frustration can ensue on both sides. It is easy for either to be derogatory about the other, blaming the other for the unpleasantness of the experience. We have already seen that perceiving another person as having much higher intelligence than our own can cause us to feel uneasy, and we have explored the different ways that this could be threatening. Perceiving another person as having much lower intelligence than your own can be similarly disconcerting, again taking you out of your comfort zone, but for different reasons.

If the discrepancy is not too marked, it might actually have the effect of making you feel better about yourself, and more capable, in relation to the other person. But where it is more severe, it can be unwelcome to have to confront that it is possible for people to have a significant impairment in the level of cognitive functioning that we ordinarily expect of each other. This can leave us not knowing how to relate to such a person, or make us feel embarrassed by ways that he or she contravenes acceptable social behaviours. We might feel sorry for such persons. We may feel unable to have the patience needed for dealing with them or feel reluctant to put in the effort that dealing with them requires. We might also be afraid of having to take on responsibility for attending to their needs. We can be left feeling bad about ourselves for having negative reactions to such people. It might also threaten our wish to be invulnerable, making us dread the prospect of losing our own level of intelligence that we automatically rely on in the way we go about our daily lives.

How do people come to have the level of intelligence that they have? Can this be increased or diminished, and if so, how? It is the search for answers to these questions, and the associated reactions and repercussions, that I am in this book arguing can be conceptualised in three main ages. The next three chapters will take us on a journey one by one through each of these three ages, also sharing along the way the main answers that have been found so far to these sorts of questions.

2

IDEALISATION OF INTELLIGENCE

In Western society, dating from long before the time when the discipline of psychology began studying intelligence scientifically, there are records of an attitude of idealisation of intelligence as an admirable, desirable human trait. This is evident in the earliest of the Ancient Greek writers: as early as around the 6th century BCE, in Homer's *Odyssey*, the ability to speak and understand well is described as an adornment from heaven that makes a person become a leader who is looked up to wherever he goes.[1] Currently, in what are accepted as valid methods of scientific research, it is considered that intelligence can be isolated as a factor from other factors and its effect on different outcomes reliably tested. But even before such methods were established, higher intelligence was associated with positive – and lower intelligence with negative – consequences of many kinds. These ranged from winning wars (the Greeks were finally victorious because of Odysseus's clever plan of the Trojan horse) to the social problems of poverty and crime (which were blamed on low intelligence).

It was during the late 19th and early 20th centuries that a growing attention to intelligence formed it into a distinct field of enquiry. Leading up to World War Two, a dominant thesis developed which accepted that higher intelligence should be systematically aspired to.

This chapter will chart the rise of that idealisation of intelligence in this pre–World War Two era – which I am calling the Age of Idealisation – and the impact it had on social policies and practices. Such policies and practices in many cases persisted well beyond World War Two, and if I cite them as examples of the pre–World-War-Two Age of Idealisation it is because they were set up during that period during which an idealisation of intelligence prevailed. Central to this thesis was a view of intelligence as something that could be objectively identified, and methods for measuring levels of human intelligence were devised.

MEASURING INTELLIGENCE IN THE AGE OF IDEALISATION

Can intelligence be measured physiologically? In the first half of the 19th century, American physician and natural scientist Samuel George Morton thought that it could be. He started with an assumption. He assumed that a person's intellectual ability was determined, proportionately, by the size of his or her brain. He then set about trying to measure different human brain sizes. He obtained the empty skulls of more than 700 corpses and measured how much internal capacity each one had by recording how many cubic inches he could fill each one with of seed, at first, and later, lead shot.[2] What he did with these cranial capacity measurements that he collated made him science's most infamous racist.

He grouped the skulls according to perceived racial divisions, calculated average measurements for each group, and then arranged the groups hierarchically in decreasing order of cranial capacity, believing this to be synonymous with decreasing order of intelligence. This was the beginning of the field of intelligence's ignominious association with racism and its focus on group differences. Group differences thinking involves categorising people into groups based on perceived differences in variables such as gender, race, and ethnicity. We will later (in Chapter 4) revisit and critique Morton's methods, as well as what I see as the spuriousness and toxicity of group differences thinking in general. In that same chapter we will also return to the question of measuring intelligence physiologically.

Not long after Morton's death in 1851, an alternative form of measurement – psychometrics – was pioneered by English polymath Francis Galton. Psychometrics seeks to measure psychologically rather than physiologically. It first originated with the specific purpose of trying to measure intelligence. The first psychometric intelligence tests that gained widespread use were those designed in 1904 by French psychologist Alfred Binet and his collaborator Theodore Simon to assess school children's levels of mental ability.

In these sorts of tests, what is being measured is not a physical characteristic but a person's performance in answering questions that require various kinds of mental effort. Such questions include manipulations and interpretations of pictures, symbols, words, and numbers. Here are a few examples.

A test of abstract reasoning often involves a sequence of images, and you have to choose from a set of images which one would complete the sequence. You achieve this by working out what the rule is that governs the sequence. This is often called "matrix reasoning". Another kind of mental effort involves remembering things. "Digit span" is a test of memory whereby a list of increasingly complex numbers is read out and you would be asked to recite back as many of the numbers as possible. Spatial ability is tested by being provided with pictures of 3D shapes which you are asked to imagine rotating by 180 degrees. For each one, you need to choose from a set of options what the resulting rotation would look like. Testing how many questions of different varieties a person can answer correctly, at what level of difficulty, and how fast, was the basis of Binet's original tests, and still is the basis of all intelligence tests.

Intelligence tests are now typically called IQ tests: IQ is an abbreviation that was first used by American professor Lewis Terman for the term Intelligence Quotient, which was coined by German psychologist William Stern. It is also Terman, who was based at Stanford University, who translated Binet's tests into English, and the Stanford-Binet Intelligence Scale – regularly updated – is still in use today. Another American psychologist, Robert Yerkes, who was based at Harvard University, first designed group-administered rather than individually administered intelligence tests. His Army Alpha test was used in the USA during World War One to select which military recruits would best be allocated to which roles.

Binet's formula for scoring his original tests was different from how intelligence tests are scored today. Recognising that children become capable of increasingly complex cognitive tasks as they get older, he categorised his test questions according to what children were typically capable of at which ages. He then scored the tests by dividing mental age by chronological age and multiplying by 100. So, if a child aged 6 could correctly accomplish tasks usually expected of a 9-year-old, then 9 divided by 6 and multiplied by 100 would give a score of 150. Conversely, if that child could not manage tasks beyond those a 3-year-old is usually capable of, their score would be 50. By this formula, a normally functioning child – a 6-year-old who performs tasks within the range that most 6-year-olds usually manage – would always have a score of 100. This system of scoring would give a clear impression of whether a child was average, or high, or low in their cognitive functioning. However, as it was based on the typical ages of child development, it was not a formula that could be applied to adults. And it is not to be confused with the contemporary statistical method of scoring IQ tests, which will be described in the next paragraph. I will keep this brief, as it makes dull reading, but it does need to be explained to enable an understanding of a few concepts and terms that will appear in subsequent pages.

Echoing the relativity of intelligence highlighted in the previous chapter, IQ scores are a measure of intelligence that is entirely relative. They show how a person who has taken a particular IQ test has performed relative to the others who took the same test under the same conditions (called a standardised test). The way this is calculated is that the score most frequently obtained is set at 100, and the standard deviation (the amount of variation there is in scores within a population) is set at 15. When the IQ scores of any general population are plotted on a graph, they form what is called a normal distribution – also called a bell curve because the graph forms the shape of an inverted bell. Such a graph enables one to see what the frequency is of any given score in that population. This can also be expressed in terms of percentiles: the percentile of a person's score means that that is the percentage of people whom that person has scored higher than. For example, an IQ score of 115 is one standard deviation above the norm, and it is on the 84th percentile.

When other human characteristics like height and weight are measured, the data also form a normal distribution. However, such characteristics are measured on a ratio scale, meaning a scale that begins at zero and increases incrementally in discrete units of universally standardised measurement. For example, height is measured in the universally standardised units of centimetres and metres or inches and feet. IQ points are not such a measurement: there is currently no ratio scale measure for human intelligence.

Just as Morton's physiological tests of intelligence rested on certain assumptions, psychometric tests also carry certain assumptions. They assume that performance on an IQ test is an accurate indication of a person's underlying level of intelligence. (As intelligence is not a phenomenon that can be directly observed, it is always being deduced from a person's behaviour.) IQ tests assume that a person's performance on that one isolated test at that moment in time has something worthwhile and enduring to say about that person's overall intellectual functioning in other contexts and at other times.

IQ tests also assume that people taking the test are trying their best, which they might well not be if they are unmotivated or are feeling distracted. Another assumption is that nothing is holding the test-taker back, which again can be untrue: a person who has dyslexia or dysgraphia, for example, will be at a disadvantage when taking a written IQ test, and that will mask their cognitive ability. I had an extremely intelligent client who performed poorly on an IQ test as a child because nobody had realised that he needed glasses: he simply couldn't see the test content properly. The topic of measuring intelligence is complex, and there is much more that can be said about it.

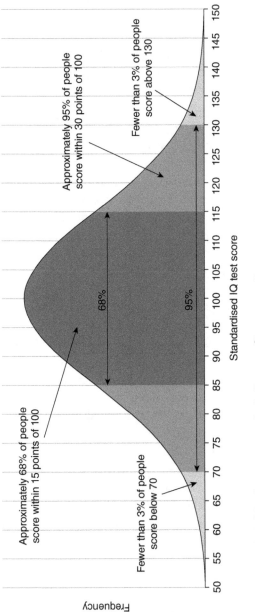

Figure 2.1 A helpful reference point: the bell curve of human intelligence

Some further points about it will be presented in Chapters 3 and 4, which will also reflect how it has developed over time.

A PROMINENT THEORY OF INTELLIGENCE ORIGINATING IN THE AGE OF IDEALISATION

The oldest modern theory of intelligence that is still in prominent use today is one that was introduced in 1904 by Charles Spearman. Spearman pioneered the statistical technique of factor analysis – also still in prominent use today – for analysing the structure of human abilities.[3] By this method he showed that when people took different cognitive performance tests, their scores across all tests would be similar to each other, or positively correlated. He termed this "positive manifold".[4]

Out of these observations he theorised that intelligence was made up of two factors. The first was a single core capability or power which he saw as giving rise to all cognitive abilities. He called this "g" for general factor of intelligence. The second he called "s-factors", referring to an array of subsidiary skills like verbal skills or mathematical skills. A person might be stronger in one specific skill than another, but all of their skills would be affected by the strength of their g.

CONFRONTING PARTICULARLY LOW INTELLIGENCE

The word "idiot" – with roots in Latin meaning an ignorant or uneducated person and in Greek meaning a person who is not fit to take part in public life – was in regular use in medieval England as a term for individuals who lacked the understanding to manage their own affairs.[5] A law titled the Prerogativa Regis allowed for the king to take over property ownership from those who were judged to be idiots by a jury of 12 men.[6] The king would take over the profits from their land but in turn provide them "their necessaries".[7] This highlights the practical implications of low intelligence: if a person does not have the intellectual capacity in adulthood to independently take care of themselves and meet their own daily needs, then those tasks have to be taken on by someone else. Attempts to address this have gone through several variations over the centuries.

The medieval practical focus on protection of and provision of care for individuals who were perceived as idiots moved during the Reformation towards a religious interpretation of their condition. This introduced moral condemnation: so-called idiots were labelled sinners who could not be saved because they had no ability to reason. In England, care of such individuals that had been taken on by their families, or by appointed guardians or monastic hospitals, from 1575 onwards started being transferred to "houses of correction" designed for criminals, called bridewells. Or, from 1697 onwards, so-called idiots were put to work as much as was possible in workhouses, which were institutions established to house the poor. Some were accommodated in private madhouses.

People who were mentally deficient were seen as subhuman and were routinely treated cruelly: no distinction was made between their condition and needs and those of other individuals who were considered deviants for other reasons. It was in the 17th century that those defined as idiots started becoming objects of curiosity for scientific study. This led to a shift, in the 18th century, towards medicalisation: from 1774 onwards, a medical certificate was required for someone seen as an idiot to be admitted to a madhouse.

In the mid-19th century the first institution specifically for idiots – the Charity for the Asylum of Idiots – was opened in London. This expressed another shift in approach: this asylum and similar others that opened later were seen as educational institutions, although medical certification was required for admission. When general compulsory elementary education was instated nationally in England in 1880, further provision became necessary for children who could not manage the syllabus that was being delivered in regular classrooms. By 1903 – the year before the introduction of Binet's first intelligence tests – the first special schools for slower learners had been established in England. The same issue had to be addressed in many other countries also, as it was around this time that compulsory education was introduced in most Western European countries. In the USA in 1911 a law was passed requiring a special class to be created whenever there were 10 or more students who were performing at a level 3 years behind their chronological ages.[8]

Whatever the different approaches have been over the centuries – practical, moral, labour-focused, scientific, medical, or education-focused – very low intelligence remains a social reality that requires a strategy for how to deal with it. How to refer to it has changed over the years, from calling it idiocy, to mental subnormality, to mental handicap, to being mentally retarded, to having a learning disability. The current internationally preferred term is "intellectual disability",[9] which is the term I will use. How intellectual disability is dealt with is of course very much influenced by what the prevailing attitude towards it is. And the prevailing attitude is also something that has changed over the ages.

DISCRIMINATING AGAINST THOSE WITH LOWER INTELLIGENCE

Once IQ tests had been devised, they were soon appropriated to point to who has intelligence and who doesn't, and in a manner that was not a neutral observation but which was judgment laden. Morton made it clear, in his hierarchy of skull sizes, that the human beings whom he identified as having the highest intelligence were best and superior to other human beings. Galton, too, openly discriminated in favour of higher intelligence and against lower intelligence, which he termed "feeble-mindedness".

In Binet's classification of levels of intelligence, his original French words for the lower levels – including "moron" and "imbecile" – soon entered into common usage even in the English language as derogatory terms, being flung as insults at people who were experienced as not understanding, being frustrating, slow, or incompetent, and thought of as stupid. Conversely, colloquial language labelled those with the highest perceived intelligence as "gifted". This term is already present in the 5th century BCE in Ancient Greek philosopher

Plato's *Republic* (Book 5).[10] It is thought to derive from the concept of high abilities being "gifts from the gods".[11]

During the Age of Idealisation, practices developed that made discrimination in favour of higher intelligence a norm. In schools, for example, such idealisation was often brazenly carried out in ways that paid no thought to the psychological, social, and emotional impact on those who were discriminated against. Or on those who were idealised.

Stanford University professor Carol Dweck described, as follows, how her grade-school teacher idealised intelligence:

> She seated us around the room in IQ order. She handed out every coveted responsibility, from clapping the blackboard erasers to carrying the flag in the assembly, on the basis of IQ. Next to our names in her roll book were our IQ scores written in large black numbers.[12]

Dweck has since extensively researched and written about how the way people are treated affects the self-concept they develop plus their subsequent behaviour around manifesting and exercising their ability.

The practices in the previous example took place in an elementary school (primary school) in the USA. What is probably the most famous senior school (high school) in the UK provides further striking examples of practices that blatantly idealise intelligence. Every year, the all-boys boarding school Eton College names 14 of the new boys joining the school as "King's Scholars" on the basis of having been the best performers in a gruelling public exam that is undertaken by hundreds. UK Prime Minister Boris Johnson was a King's Scholar, as was British writer Harry Eyres. Eyres remembers how the King's Scholars felt intellectually superior to the other 1,200 boys, from whom they were very visibly set apart by living in separate quarters in the old core of the College and wearing special gowns.

During each school year at Eton extensive tests were administered to all the students, and if you didn't pass, your test paper would be held up in class by the teacher and literally ripped in two. This was called "a rip" and had to be signed by your house master and private tutor. Doing very well, on the other hand, was termed a "show up", which had to be similarly signed. But an even more public drawing of attention to ability took place in what has been called a "barbaric" ritual[13] that involved the giving out of the results of examinations named "trials".

Rather than taking place in individual classes, for trials results all pupils in the year block – about 250 – would troop into a large hall. There the lower master – an imposing figure wearing a black gown – would read out loud where each boy's results placed him in relation to the others. He would start with the name of the one who came lowest and then read out all the rest of the names and positions in reverse order. The person who came last was awarded the title of "GTF", for "General Total Failure". No thought was given to the humiliation such a ritual caused for those who came lowest, what egotism it could encourage in those who came highest, or what divisiveness was thereby created amongst the pupils. Or perhaps these were precisely the outcomes desired: to shame the lower achievers, aggrandise the higher achievers, and intensify a divided society.

One portrayal of how the idealisation of intelligence could be taken to an ultimate extreme can be found in the science fiction television series *Star Trek*. Here characters are depicted who have evolved to no longer needing anything more than – or even being anything more than – a functioning brain. Becoming a disembodied intelligence is the utmost depiction of nothing mattering except the workings of the intellect, which are elevated above all else.

RESEARCH FOCUSING ON HOW TO INCREASE INTELLIGENCE

Intelligence research during the Age of Idealisation might not quite have been seeking how to bring the *Star Trek* vision into reality, but it was certainly driven by the question of how to increase intelligence.

There was a recognition of the burden placed on society by very low intelligence, as well as a recognition that positive contributions to society through knowledge acquisition, innovation, and leadership were associated with the competence of high intelligence. Underlying the question of how to increase intelligence is the question of what causes intelligence to be low or high.

An early (16th-century) account of what caused very low intelligence was that of the changeling myth. This held that the devil had stolen the perfect child and replaced it with his own offspring.[14] Causes now known about include problems during birth that deprive the brain of oxygen, genetic disorders like Down Syndrome or Fragile X Syndrome, and illnesses such as meningitis.

In terms of high intelligence, in the 19th century Galton produced the first major empirical study of genius.[15] By applying statistical analysis to a study he conducted of 1,000 eminent men from 300 families, he demonstrated that certain families produced several geniuses over many generations whereas other families did not produce any individuals of note. In his book *Hereditary Genius* (1869)[16] he asserted that this proved that intelligence was a genetically inherited trait. He was the first person to use the phrase "nature versus nurture" which is now so commonly used in debates about, respectively, genetic influences versus environmental influences.

Galton was influenced by his famous half-cousin Charles Darwin's groundbreaking work *On the Origin of Species*, published in 1859.[17] Darwin showed how animal species evolved to improve their fitness for survival by means of the physical characteristics that were most beneficial for survival becoming naturally selected to be reproduced. Applying this thinking to humans, Galton considered that humans would increase their fitness for survival by increasing their intelligence. And he considered that the most efficient way to increase intelligence in society would be to assist natural selection by intervening to steer people with high intelligence to have more children and those with low intelligence to have no children.

CULMINATION OF THE AGE OF IDEALISATION IN EUGENICS

I see the era of idealising intelligence as having culminated in eugenics, with its peak being during World War Two. The most notorious example of eugenics is that of the policies and practices of Nazi Germany. These involved mass identification and extermination of people who were deemed inferior on the basis of intellectual functioning, ethnicity, disability, or sexual orientation.

It all started in 1883 with Galton coining the term eugenics by combining the Greek words *eu* (good) and *genos* (birth).[18] In the early 20th century Galton's ideas about how to improve society through selective breeding were optimistically taken up and – with embellishments that Galton had not himself advocated – put into practice by many countries around the world through the introduction of eugenic social policies.

Eugenic policies legislated ways of encouraging procreation in target populations, termed positive eugenics. For example, the British government introduced tax breaks for highly educated couples to have more children.[19] Negative eugenics involved segregating unwanted individuals and preventing them from reproducing. For example, American psychologist Henry Herbert Goddard was instrumental in developing immigration controls that prevented entry into the USA of individuals who were deemed feeble-minded: intelligence tests were administered at New York's Ellis Island checkpoint and used to turn thousands away over a period of 40 years.[20] Forced sterilisation of those judged intellectually inferior became widespread in the USA, Canada, Mexico, and several Western and East Central European countries. Eugenics represents a peak in the belief that where intelligence is concerned, nature overrides nurture.

Although Galton's work focused on intelligence, eugenics soon extended to encompass other traits that were decided to be undesirable. South Africa became infamous for its race-based laws, the first of which were published in 1910. These were later extended into the full *apartheid* regime. *Apartheid* openly claimed certain races to be less intelligent than, and therefore inferior to, others, and routed people into separate residential areas, separate public amenities, and separate educational systems based entirely on their physiological features such as the colour of their skin. Inter-marriage – and even sexual relations – between the different classified races was forbidden. And, of course, in the case of Nazi Germany there was not only forced segregation, or forced sterilisation, of those who were discriminated against, but forced extermination.

THE PSYCHOLOGY UNDERLYING THE AGE OF IDEALISATION

This phase of idealisation has its roots in three of our most primitive psychological processes. It involves the making of ideals that we can aspire to, splitting things into good versus bad, and tribalistically dividing in-groups (which we accept and want to belong with) from out-groups (those to be rejected and even destroyed).

When we are children we all – in many subtle ways as well as explicitly – are repeatedly presented with the visions our parents hold of what ideal behaviour is and ideal thoughts, ideal habits, and ideal pursuits. These ideals provide guidelines for us of what is expected of us, what will be praised, and what will be punished. We all grow up being told to be a good girl or good boy. We get rewarded when we are said to have been good. When we do not comply with these guidelines, we get told that we have been bad, or that we are bad, and we experience being disapproved of and scolded. We tend to adopt these taught ideals, at least initially, because we learn that by doing so we are assured of receiving the affection, protection, and provisions that we need for our survival and well-being.

How affected we are by close relationships is what has been extensively studied in attachment theory. This is a body of knowledge, pioneered by John Bowlby,[21] that has demonstrated with decades of empirical research[22] that humans are genetically programmed to seek safety – a "secure base" – by building close enduring relationships with others, beginning with those on whom we are reliant for our care during infancy and childhood. Taking in the ideals of those who are important to us creates for us the safety of knowing how to gain their approval, but also creates fear of what the consequences will be if we fall short of what is expected of us. Eventually we participate in setting our own ideals: having something to strive for gives our lives structure and meaning.

As well as having regular experiences of how others (parents, teachers, peers) divide our behaviour into good and bad, in turn we divide our own feelings about ourselves and others, and our evaluations of our own and their behaviour, into good and bad. Good is associated with safety, and bad with fearful consequences. Psychoanalytic thinkers, particularly Melanie Klein,[23] have described how we try to keep ourselves feeling safe and ward off anxiety by trying always to see ourselves and those whom we need to be closely involved with as good. We do this by splitting away from the good anything that we perceive as bad – which we fear – and by trying to get rid of it.

Behaviours associated with intelligence universally align with typically held ideals: showing an acquiring of knowledge, learning from experience, giving good answers to questions, and solving problems all usually attract approving responses. When we are children and we exhibit such behaviours we get told we have done well, which makes us feel good about ourselves. Getting things wrong can easily make us feel bad about ourselves. Experiencing negative reactions to getting things wrong can make us fear getting things wrong.

One way of preserving the feeling that you are in the safe zone of being good is to be able to locate what is perceived as bad outside of yourself, in others. We all have primitive fears of being judged inadequate and being rejected. If we can expel those qualities from ourselves and project them onto someone else instead who can be pointed to as the one who is inadequate, then we can feel by comparison exonerated and safe. That person can, instead of us, be the one who is rejected. This is what children are doing when they feel threatened and say it wasn't me, it was him. I'm the good one, she's the bad one.

Do you remember, when you were at school, there being an "in crowd"? Can you think of examples of how individuals who were within, versus outside of, that group, were perceived and treated? When we can create a group within which we agree that those of us together in that group are good, that makes all the members of the group feel even more safe. And this safety can be further secured by projecting all that is perceived as bad onto other groups. Social identity theory[24] has shown that the mere existence of a categorisation of a group as separate and other than the group you are in (the in-group) leads to discrimination against that other group as an out-group. This is not based on maximising profits to the in-group but is based on maximising differences in the out-group. In other words, discrimination is based on emphasising that those in the out-group are different.

When particular characteristics come to be associated with a particular person or group, this easily leads to widely held but fixed and oversimplified images or ideas of what that type of person or group is like: in other words, it leads to the forming of stereotypes. Stereotyping a group as containing the ones who are bad serves the purpose for us of getting rid of the bad that we want to remove from us and locating it in them. However, it also then leaves us feeling afraid of those others whom we now see as being all bad. The apartheid laws of South Africa were entirely based on trying to suppress races who, at that time, in that social context, were powerfully feared. And, similarly, during the Age of Idealisation those with very low IQ came to be feared: "[t]he multiplication of the feeble-minded is a very terrible danger to the race" – so wrote British statesman Winston Churchill in a memo to the prime minister in 1910.[25] From here it is a natural psychological progression to start to advise that in the interests of our own safety, those who are so dangerous should be eliminated.

HOW THE AGE OF IDEALISATION CAME TO AN END

I am marking as the end of the Age of Idealisation the ending of eugenics practices and policies that were coercive and carried out at the population level. It is generally considered that it was following World War Two's conclusion in 1945 that such eugenics ended.[26] Events that are taken as the marker of this are the Nuremburg Trials (German doctors being tried for war crimes) and the Convention for the Prevention and Punishment of the Crime of Genocide (or Genocide Convention), which was unanimously adopted by the United Nations General Assembly in 1948. However, the retraction of eugenics practices and policies took time to put into effect. Any big social change takes considerable time to be established. Over the next decades, organisations in Europe, Australia, Britain, Canada, and America all changed their names from titles that included the words "eugenics" and "hygiene" (mental hygiene, racial hygiene) to titles related mostly to "family planning" and "genetics".[27]

The practices of Hitler's Nazis demonstrated the furthest excesses of the atrocities of eugenics. Many millions of people were exterminated for other perceived defects also, not only related to intelligence, but many tens of thousands of these deaths are attributed directly to intelligence-based prejudice.[28] This caused such worldwide shock that it heralded a new era, a backlash against the idealisation of intelligence.

3

DEVALUATION OF INTELLIGENCE

In the aftermath of World War Two, conscience-stricken societies sought to create distance away from any of the sorts of values that had been exalted in Hitler's prejudices and enacted with his deadly policies. This meant that the thesis of idealising intelligence that had characterised the pre-World War Two era, and which underpinned many eugenics practices, now came to be reacted to with its opposite. An antithesis now developed that involved a growing denigration or devaluation of intelligence. I am calling this second phase the Age of Devaluation. Although during the Age of Devaluation there was still evidence of intelligence being an esteemed and sought-after trait, such an attitude came more and more to be frowned upon and deterred from being openly displayed. Gradually a paradigm shift became apparent that distinguished it from the Age of Idealisation.

The ethos of the Age of Devaluation is that those who struggle must be elevated, leaving those who shine intellectually to feel somewhat ashamed and be hidden away. Intelligence research is seen as increasingly suspicious, safer to be stayed away from. Even teaching intelligence comes to be seen as too tricky and ceases to be attempted in many universities.[1] Public opinion blanketly vilifies those who had looked at head sizes as a measure of intelligence or who had ever believed or disseminated any of the data related to such a practice, such a "Mismeasure of Man". That was the title of a bestselling and award-winning book by Stephen Jay Gould[2] (more about which will be said later) which I see as being emblematic of the Age of Devaluation. Most of the headings of this chapter match the headings used in the previous chapter, in the same order, so as to document how the same issues that have been introduced in relation to the Age of Idealisation developed differently in the Age of Devaluation.

MEASURING INTELLIGENCE IN THE AGE OF DEVALUATION

We have seen how it was during the Age of Idealisation that IQ tests came to be settled upon as a method for measuring human intelligence. Their popularity had soared: the National Intelligence Test published in the USA in 1919 sold over half a million copies in a year[3] for use in schools, universities, and businesses. In contrast, by the Age of Devaluation the use – and misuse – of IQ tests had acquired such negative associations of elitism and racism that test producers started to deny that it was intelligence that their tests were evaluating. To avoid controversy and increase marketability they started calling their products tests of *aptitude* or *ability* instead of tests of intelligence.[4]

During the Age of Devaluation the measuring of intelligence was widely attacked. Popular criticisms of IQ tests included that what they measure is far too narrow to be able to be said to reflect a person's intelligence; that such tests are culturally biased – not culture fair – and therefore disadvantage test-takers who do not, for example, share the mother tongue of the test-makers; and that test results can be inaccurate because of stereotype threat. Stereotype threat refers to individuals performing worse than they have the capability of performing when they are members of a group (based on age, gender, race, or socioeconomic status) that has been stereotyped as being unsuccessful.[5]

A good representation of the wish during this era to devalue the measuring of intelligence can be seen in a paper published in 1979 with the title "Bad News Concerning IQ Tests".[6] The bad news being reported was that evidence had been found that IQ tests were not biased racially or socioeconomically. It is clear from the title that the authors of this paper recognised that their research findings would not be welcomed.

THREE PROMINENT THEORIES OF INTELLIGENCE ORIGINATING IN THE AGE OF DEVALUATION

There were theorists, too, who tried to move away from the way intelligence had so far been conceptualised and measured. Robert Sternberg's 1985 book *Beyond IQ: A Triarchic Theory of Human Intelligence*[7] identified three aspects to intelligence, only one of which is targeted in IQ tests. In the 1990s, he evolved this thinking into what he named his theory of successful intelligence,[8] which contained the same three aspects from his triarchic theory but described in more accessible language.

The three aspects identified by Sternberg were what he called analytical intelligence, practical intelligence, and creative intelligence. He explained analytical intelligence broadly as involving the capacity to analyse what a good solution to a problem would be. He related this to traditional academic ability, which is what IQ tests focus on. However, he stressed that such a capacity on its own would not lead to a person achieving success in life. For this, what would be needed is two further capacities: the capacity to generate worthwhile problems to solve (novel and useful ideas), which he saw as creative intelligence, and the capacity to make solutions work and be accepted by others, which he saw as practical intelligence. But how would you define "success in life"?

Sternberg defined success in life in completely relative terms – "given one's personal standards, within one's sociocultural context".[9] So according to this, Galileo Galilei (see Chapter 1), who I'm sure we would agree showed signs of having strong general intelligence, would not qualify as having Sternberg's "successful intelligence". This is because his ideas – whilst correct – were ahead of his time, and he refused to give up on them and adapt to his sociocultural context, no matter how impractical that was, causing him to have to spend the rest of his life under house arrest. Was his behaviour unintelligent, do you think?

Out of all theories of intelligence, the one that is probably most well-known is one which originated during the Age of Devaluation: it is Howard Gardner's theory of multiple intelligences. With this Gardner newly named several non-cognitive abilities as kinds of intelligence. He started by designating seven different areas of human functioning as separate intelligences: linguistic; logical-mathematical; spatial; musical; bodily-kinaesthetic (an aptitude for physical movement, such as is seen in, for example, a skilled ballet dancer); interpersonal (relating to social skills); and intrapersonal (involving self-awareness and self-understanding).[10] Later, he added two further intelligences: naturalistic (an empathy for phenomena in the natural world) and existential (which is similar to spiritual awareness and insight).[11] Only the first three of these nine so-called intelligences overlap with what is assessed in traditional intelligence tests. Even later, Gardner yet again added two more: mental searchlight intelligence (a capacity for scanning wider systems and providing leadership in these) and laser intelligence (this involves a narrower specialisation in a particular art, science, or trade).[12] One way of devaluing the concept of intelligence is precisely to create a glut of intelligences, whereby almost any kind of activity is defined as a kind of intelligence, with more and more of them being added.

The theories of Gardner and Sternberg were widely welcomed for diverging from the traditional cognitive focus, and they have had strong social and cultural support and impact. However, whilst very popular with the general public, they are less well regarded in the scientific world: they lack the empirical support that g theory has. Theories of intelligence that focus on the components that are involved in performance on intelligence tests are termed psychometric theories (psychometric meaning psychological measurement), and Gardner's and Sternberg's theories do not have this focus. Their theories, therefore, are not psychometric theories of intelligence.

Turning to psychometric theories, a prominent psychometric theory of intelligence that originated during this era is the Cattell-Horn theory of fluid intelligence versus crystallised intelligence. This was first published by Raymond Bernard Cattell and his student John Horn in the 1960s.[13] This theory defines fluid intelligence, or Gf, as the ability to come up with a fresh analysis and solution of new and unusual problems. This is differentiated from crystallised intelligence, or Gc, which is the ability to apply previously acquired knowledge to current problems. Since being modified by John Carroll in the 1990s[14] it is sometimes referred to as Cattell-Horn-Carroll (CHC) theory or as the three-stratum model of intelligence.[15]

DISCRIMINATING AGAINST THOSE WITH HIGHER INTELLIGENCE

In the previous chapter we saw examples of how an Age of Idealisation ethos manifested in school rituals that very publicly drew attention to intelligence and academic achievement. Such rituals were simply part of the ordinary school day. In the Age of Devaluation, however, in some schools even special occasions that only took place once a year – such as prize-giving – were altered so as to be downplayed, demonstrating how those who shine came to be hidden away. For example, the award-winning Highgate School in London changed its annual prize-giving ceremony to make it a less public event so that only the winning pupils and their families would attend. This ensures that no-one who is not getting a prize has to suffer attention being drawn to the fact that there are others who have done better than they have.

Not only academic achievement, but achievement in general underwent a cultural revision during the Age of Devaluation. Many junior and senior schools in the UK also changed their annual sports day events so that traditions of individuals competing against each other for rewards of cups or medals were replaced with team activities that emphasised being commended for taking part. This mimics the words of the Dodo in *Alice's Adventures in Wonderland*: "*Everybody* has won, and all must have prizes".[16]

During the Age of Devaluation the general ethos of education came to be about identifying those who are struggling and helping them to improve their attainment. It is still apparent in almost any text on education that there is an unquestioned assumption that resources need to be devoted to this. There is almost never a corresponding representation of it being important to help those who can more easily do well – or who are doing well – to do better, to do their best. In 2010 the UK's Gifted and Talented Programme was discontinued, diverting the budget instead to help socioeconomically disadvantaged young people get into university.

Some universities made it clear that they were not interested in trying to recruit high-IQ prospective students because this was too small a population to be of financial interest to them. They deliberately aimed their marketing strategy at academically average groups. They reasoned that these groups incorporated a higher proportion of students and therefore could yield the recruiting of higher numbers of students.

Once students had been recruited, those who were not doing well on their courses would be offered one-to-one mentoring to help improve their results. Again there was a financial motivation, to try to lower the attrition rate (the dropping-out of lower-performing students) and with that the loss of student fees. However, such policies discriminate against higher-achieving students because those students are paying the same tuition fees but are not being offered the same opportunities for extra one-to-one attention to improve their performance. If mentoring were offered to other groups of students it might help move a medium-performing student into gaining a distinction, or help challenge a first-class student to develop their potential more fully, beyond grade-oriented goals. But funding for the mentoring scheme was only made available to target lower-achieving students, and none was made available to any other student groups.

Age of Devaluation attitudes of discrimination against higher intelligence are visible wherever derogatory comments are made about high intelligence. For example, a journalist wrote that what was needed to gain membership of the international high-IQ society Mensa was a very high Intelligence Quotient. And then she added, "You also, I imagine, have to have a higher than average Insufferable Quotient".[17]

An example of the devaluation of intelligence being taken to an extreme is seen in evolutionary psychologist Satoshi Kanazawa's (2012) book *The Intelligence Paradox*.[18] He argues that individuals with very high IQ are "stupid", have "stupid preferences", are ill-equipped for "the most important things in life", and are "the ultimate losers in life". He of course defines what he means by all of this, but he blithely uses these derogatory descriptors for a portion of the population whom he has singled out entirely on the basis of their high intelligence. It leaves one with the impression that high intelligence is a somewhat ridiculous evolutionary anomaly that is worth mocking, and that can freely be mocked with no opprobrium.

RESEARCH ON INTELLIGENCE SHUNNED

During the Age of Devaluation there was a swing towards dismissing research into intelligence in general as being negative. This has been termed a "controversialisation"[19] of the field of intelligence. Researchers who arrived at scientific findings about intelligence that were socially unpopular experienced "hostile media coverage and politicized misrepresentation of their research".[20] Such researchers included Arthur Jensen, Charles Murray, and Linda Gottfredson.[21]

Often what was being reacted to was anything that stated intelligence to be a genetically inherited trait, as the statement of such a fact was conflated with racism because of Age of Idealisation policies and practices. A study showed that there was a dramatic rise in the frequency with which there appeared in a wide variety of publications the word "intelligence" or "IQ" in the same sentence as the word "racism" or "racist".[22] This study looked at the period between 1965 and 2000, which falls firmly within what I am defining as the Age of Devaluation.

One researcher who became the centre of a heated controversy is Raymond Bernard Cattell, mentioned previously for his theory on fluid versus crystallised intelligences. The American Psychological Foundation (APF) recognised him as one of the most eminent psychologists of the 20th century, with a Gold Medal Award for Life Achievement in Psychological Science. In August 1997 – at the age of 92 – Cattell travelled from Hawaii to Chicago to receive this award.[23] However, political activists threatened to disrupt the proceedings if he was given the award, because during his career he had supported eugenics. The APF responded to this pressure by deciding to postpone the award ceremony. Cattell acted tactfully to dissipate the situation by announcing that he was declining the award. This happened what turned out to be six months before his death in February 1998. What this incident shows is how the tide had turned on the Age of Idealisation, which Cattell was associated with. Scientific work that had been significant enough to be commended in a lifetime achievement award was now rejected.

An impact of this controversialisation of intelligence within the overall swing to an Age of Devaluation was that research on intelligence was thwarted. Or where research was still undertaken, its scope was narrowed so as to stay away from problematic topics. This thwarting was enacted through such researchers facing difficulty getting their work funded and/or published, suffering withdrawal of social support from colleagues and withdrawal of institutional resources, and even in certain cases experiencing dismissal from jobs and threats of violence from political activists.[24]

These developments towards viewing intelligence as a suspicious topic and thwarting intelligence research also led to universities ceasing to offer courses on intelligence for fear of causing offence.[25] A study in 2014 on the content of psychology textbooks and course curricula showed that the space devoted to the subject of intelligence had dropped from 6% of textbook space in the 1980s to 4% in the 21st century.[26] Previously there would be a full chapter on intelligence, but this had ceased to be the case, with intelligence instead being fitted into other sections such as on language and thought.

RISE OF FOCUS ON EMOTIONAL INTELLIGENCE

The 1990s saw the beginning of what has become an increasingly ubiquitous counterbalance to the Age of Idealisation's idealising of cognitive intelligence. It started with Daniel Goleman's book *Emotional Intelligence*, which declared in its subtitle *Why It Can Matter More Than IQ*.[27] Emotional intelligence, often represented as "EQ" or sometimes as "EI", refers to a person's capacity to be aware of, understand, manage, and express their own emotions, and to understand and manage others' emotions with empathy and effective social skills. During the Age of Devaluation popular support for the theory of emotional intelligence, together with popular support for Gardner's theory of multiple intelligences, burgeoned, well ahead of empirical support for either of these theories: educational web sites representing these theories increased at ten times the rate of increase of professional journal articles on these theories.[28]

As the concept of emotional intelligence gained potency, a common criticism of high-IQ people came to be that they do not have much emotional intelligence. This would often be expressed by people in general conversation as though it were pleasing to have been able to find that flaw, and as though it was a flaw that ruled out the worth of the cognitive intelligence. One author called high-IQ individuals "clever sillies", saying that they had socially inappropriate behaviour and that this was the case because they lacked common sense.[29] Such criticisms would usually be expressed as though people who lacked emotional intelligence were themselves to blame for it, as though they ought to be more emotionally intelligent and not being more so was due to a failing of their own.

CULMINATION OF THE AGE OF DEVALUATION IN EXPERTISE

I see the era of devaluing intelligence as having culminated in the establishment of the field of expertise with its assertion that there are no differences in innate cognitive ability and that anyone can achieve anything so long as they engage in enough "deliberate practise".[30] A figure was even put on what counts as enough: "10,000 hours". These terms in quotation marks derive from the work of Swedish psychologist and researcher Anders Ericsson, who has published prolifically and whose ideas were referred to and repeated in a number of popular books that appeared between 2008 and 2014.[31] Probably the most well-known of these is Malcolm Gladwell's (2008) "No. 1 international bestseller" *Outliers: The Story of Success*.[32] Ericsson's work, and all the publications echoing him, stress that no innate ability is needed for expertise acquisition, and that there are no inborn differences in mental ability (only in physical ability which affects sporting performance). With regard to the nature versus nurture debate, this constitutes the apotheosis of nurture triumphing over nature.

These views as expressed by Ericsson and Gladwell and others came to be widely propagated in both mainstream and academic literature, widely influencing policies and practices. For example, in his book *The Expert Learner*,[33] Gordon Stobart, a professor affiliated with some of the top universities in the UK, declared that the idea of innate variation in ability was a myth and urged educational institutions to reconstruct their assumptions about this. Other professors in the UK, USA, and Australia strongly endorsed his views, recommending this as "the one book" that "all teachers, parents, employers and politicians who are interested in education should read".[34]

THE PSYCHOLOGY UNDERLYING THE AGE OF DEVALUATION

The underlying psychological motivation in the Age of Devaluation is that of guilt at the previous era's discrimination. Guilt is felt about the way that intelligence was idealised, and shame is felt at the excesses and atrocities that such idealisation led to. Seeking to compensate for this, however, provoked discrimination the other way around. The attempt to rectify discrimination against low intelligence developed into discrimination against high intelligence, causing a devaluing of intelligence and promoting a culture of anti-intellectualism.

Trying to compensate for discrimination against one party by simply reversing it and making the opposite party the target of discrimination instead is a typical reaction, which creates an ongoing cycle of discrimination. This is what Nelson Mandela presciently, wisely, and with extraordinary compassion urged against when – following having been imprisoned by the *apartheid* regime for 29 years – he became South Africa's first black state president. He knew that the wish to compensate those who had been discriminated against would be strong and could easily provoke discrimination the other way around. But he wanted to end the cycle of discrimination. He therefore urged against retaliation. Instead, he pressed for reconciliation.

When recognising and wanting to rectify discrimination, there is a drive to rule out unfairness. The deeply held wish for fairness translates into a moral value and a political creed that we should all be equal. Concentrating on this can make us susceptible to faulty reasoning. An example of this is what has been termed the "moralistic fallacy".[35] This is the kind of error in logic we make when we believe that because something *should be* a certain way, it *is* that way. So, where intelligence is concerned, because we value intelligence and believe that we all *should* be equal in ways that we value, we then believe that we all *are* equal in intelligence. It is fully acceptable to acknowledge that certain individual differences in humans exist – such as differences in height or sporting ability. These are accepted as a reality that is to be expected. However, a perception that there are differences between individuals in intellectual ability is something that in the Age of Devaluation came to be increasingly rejected as unpalatable. What makes us able to think clearly where individual differences like height are involved, yet fall prey to the moralistic fallacy where intelligence is involved?

The answer is that our ability to think clearly gets clouded when emotion is triggered. When emotion is involved, reason, or logic, can get overruled.[36] Individual differences such as height are (generally) non-threatening, so an emotional reaction to such differences is not triggered, allowing logic to prevail. But intelligence is not non-threatening, so emotion becomes engaged. The reasons that intelligence can generally be threatening have been outlined in Chapter 1's section "Our Fear of Intelligence", but these reasons were vastly augmented by the Age of Idealisation's policies and practices. During the Age of Idealisation it was a very real threat that you could be put to death because of not being intelligent enough, and there is no greater threat than that. I see the situation in which intelligence came to be seen, as one author put it, as "the most important trait that any human can have",[37] as being a direct consequence of the Age of Idealisation.

Tied up with fairness and retaliation is another part of our psychology, which the paradigm shift in the Age of Devaluation gave free reign to, and that is envy. Envy is what we feel towards others whom we see as having some sort of advantage that we do not have (how unfair!). Envy makes us want to spoil that advantage: it is as though we feel that the person we envy has done something unpleasant in relation to us that we have an urge to retaliate against. Seeing someone as having an advantage can automatically make us feel worse about ourselves in relation to that person, which makes us feel negatively about them. As Irish playwright and wit Oscar Wilde said, "The public is wonderfully tolerant. It forgives everything except genius".[38]

Conversely, if we see that someone else is suffering, we definitely do not have to envy that person, so we automatically feel better about ourselves in relation to them. This is encapsulated in the German term *Schadenfreude*, which has been happily adopted in the English-speaking world: *Schadenfreude* means the taking of pleasure at another's misfortune. Cultural historian Tiffany Watt Smith[39] shows that many other cultures have similar terms:

> The Japanese have a saying: "The misfortunes of others taste like honey". The French speak of *joie maligne*, a diabolical delight in other people's suffering. The Danish talk of *skadefryd*, and the Dutch of *leedvermaak*. In Hebrew enjoying other people's catastrophes is *simcha la-ed*. . . . More than two thousand years ago . . . the Greeks described *epichairekakia* (literally *epi*, over, *chairo*, rejoice, *kakia*, disgrace). "To see others suffer does one good", wrote the philosopher Friedrich Nietzsche.

Smith cites a reader of the *New York Times* in 2008 as having lamented that we are living in "a Golden Age of *Schadenfreude*", and she cites a commentator in the UK newspaper *The Guardian* who termed it a "Spitegeist".[40] These could well be apt synonyms for what I have designated as the Age of Devaluation.

The expertise antithesis, as a reaction against the thesis of idealising intelligence, is very popular. It makes everyone feel better about themselves because if no-one has innately higher ability than anyone else, then we don't have to feel envious of anyone for having higher ability than ourselves. We don't have to fear inadequacy in our own ability, because we have been convinced that anyone who works hard enough can achieve anything. If we believe others have only succeeded because they have worked very hard for it, we can also release our envy by mocking them for their work – swot! Nerd! Teacher's pet! These names, used in a derogatory way, would during the Age of Devaluation be flung with impunity at high achievers. No parallels seem to have been drawn – or bothered about – between such behaviour and the names low achievers would be called during the Age of Idealisation (moron, idiot, imbecile), which by the Age of Devaluation had become censured.

Believing that those who succeed only did so by working much harder fulfils what Australian researcher Norman Feather[41] identified as the excusing criterion of deservingness. If we believe someone deserves something, then we do not see it as being unfair. We can feel happy about someone's success – quelling our envy – if we believe they deserve their success because they worked very hard for it, and preferably were disadvantaged to start with, rags to riches. The only problem with this is that this depiction of expertise is not entirely true.

HOW THE AGE OF DEVALUATION CAME TO AN END

Anyone who has ever watched any group of individuals who are of the same age applying themselves to the same task will have noticed that there is variability amongst them in performance. And is that purely because they had received dissimilar amounts of tutoring in that task or had engaged in dissimilar amounts of practise? Many of the books that propagated the view that anyone can achieve anything if enough effort is exerted can be found to contain – unwittingly, one suspects – details in the same book that contradict that view. I'll give an example from Daniel Coyle's book *The Talent Code*.[42]

Coyle asserts very strongly and repetitively that there is no such thing as talent and that anyone who works hard enough, and knows what to work on, will be able to succeed. He tells the story of voice coach Linda Septien, who started out as a singer herself and who studied in meticulous detail everything that is involved in successful singing performance. By applying everything that she studied to students whom she took on and coached in singing, some of her students (such as Jessica Simpson) became famously successful performing artists. However, even though she knew all about what details need to be worked on and how to work on them, Coyle writes, "Despite all this work Septien's singing career failed to lift off over the next few years".[43] If knowing what to work on, and working very hard on it, is all that is needed for success, then surely it makes no sense that Septien's own singing career failed?

Proponents of the expertise view do not acknowledge that in spite of knowledge and hard work, some do not succeed (like Septien), yet others do (like some of her students). It also simply does not make sense that when someone did extraordinarily well at something, it was attributed purely to deliberate practise – it was denied that something such as giftedness/intellectual agility existed – yet intellectual disability continued to be named in psychiatric diagnostic manuals as a condition that did exist.[44] Manifestations of intellectual disability were not seen as a mere absence of deliberate practise.

Such contradiction can further be seen in the fact that even though the dominant idea in the Age of Devaluation was that social skills, effort, and deliberate practise were of much greater importance than intelligence, there continued to be manifestations of a keen pursuit of intelligence. Many schools, universities, and businesses continued to use assessments highly similar to IQ tests to offer places to those who attained the best results. Another striking example is that in the 1990s a report in the journal *Nature* was slightly misrepresented in wide media coverage as having provided proof that IQ could be enhanced by simply listening to Mozart.[45] Far from this being of no consequence and ignored because IQ had been discredited, it actually triggered a 17-year-long trend (before being conclusively disproven) of parents, educationalists, and even budget holders in government enthusiastically investing in recordings of Mozart in their wish to achieve this "Mozart Effect".

I see the Age of Devaluation as being brought to an end by the accumulation of growing evidence against the claims – however popular they had been – that there was no innate difference in intelligence amongst different people and that intelligence had no impact on performance. Publications that made such claims – such as Leon Kamin's *The Science and Politics of IQ* – were refuted.[46] Gould's hugely influential book, mentioned at the beginning of this chapter, which also argued against research findings on individual differences in intelligence, has since been discredited on the grounds of politically motivated "systematic misrepresentation and dishonest presentation of data".[47] More and more evidence started gathering that refuted Ericsson's views, and he too was accused of having misrepresented his research findings.[48]

In order to nominate a marker in time for the end of this devaluation phase, I am taking the turning point as being the 2014 publication of a special issue of the journal *Intelligence*[49] which was dedicated to interrogating the concept of expertise. It presented research that showed that in both chess and music – the two domains most concentrated upon in the field of expertise – deliberate practise alone was not sufficient to achieve expert performance. The research showed that performance was contributed to independently by practise and by IQ and that expert performance was highly dependent on higher IQ.

The rule that 10,000 hours of practise – said to equate to 10 years of intensive practise – is needed to acquire expertise is clearly not true of child prodigies who achieve exceptional musical performance well before they have even reached 10 years of age.[50] An example is a 6-year-old American musical prodigy who, at the time of being studied in 2003, had received no formal musical lessons or engaged in deliberate practise, but through his ability to remember melodies and recreate them he had played in numerous concerts, appeared several times on national television, been in two movies, and released two CDs in which he sings in two languages and plays several musical instruments.[51] His scores on all sections of the Stanford-Binet Intelligence Scale were much higher than average.

Supplementary to these arguments that deliberate practise alone is not all that is required for expertise acquisition, other research showed that with the same amount of practise, individuals achieve differently, and that practise actually increases the differences between individuals.[52] A study of 120 classical composers showed that there was an average amount of time that it took to acquire expertise, but that those composers who acquired expertise in less than the average time became more eminent and more prolific and had longer productive careers.[53] This showed that time spent practising could actually be inversely proportional to accomplishment.

If the expertise paradigm is not accurate, or at least not the full story, then a different way of looking at things is needed that can make sense of what the true reality is. This prompts the search for a new paradigm that can accommodate the greater complexities we have so far encountered. That is what will be explored in the next chapter.

4

INTEGRATION OF NEURODIVERSITY

We have seen in the previous two chapters how the thesis of idealising intelligence, which characterised the pre–World War Two period, made way for its antithesis in a devaluation of intelligence after World War Two. Each of these two eras culminated in significant social change, involving alterations in behaviour patterns and cultural values and norms that yielded profound social consequences. The Age of Idealisation culminated in eugenics, with its nature-based ideals for a better society and its atrocities. The Age of Devaluation culminated in widespread circulation, adoption, and application of Anders Ericsson's nurture-based theory of expertise, with its attendant inspirations and misconceptions. Neither the Age of Idealisation nor the Age of Devaluation provided viable long-term attitudes and practices in relation to human intelligence that are both humane and realistic. Each of these two ages created a paradigm – paradigms that stand in direct opposition to each other – and took it to its excess.

The visionary poet William Blake wrote that "the road of excess leads to the palace of wisdom".[1] If we can learn the lessons from the excesses of the Age of Idealisation and the Age of Devaluation, we can create a synthesis out of their opposing positions and seek a balance, a middle way. (In Buddhism, it is the middle way that finds enlightenment, rejecting extremes and "black-and-white" thinking and replacing these with more nuanced insight.) This chapter will consider how such a synthesis can be created, leading to a third age – an Age of Integration – which shows signs of already having begun. I will argue that the path towards integration involves a straightforward and non-discriminatory acknowledgment and acceptance that one of the ways in which people are different from each other is in levels of intelligence. Intelligence is simply one of many aspects of human diversity, and an aspect that I will explain as belonging within the category of "neurodiversity". But first, the chapter will start by revisiting central issues that were introduced in the preceding two chapters to show where we have got to with those as we enter an Age of Integration.

MEASURING INTELLIGENCE IN THE AGE OF INTEGRATION

By the 21st century, techniques for investigating the physiological basis of intelligence have moved on a lot. Instead of the 19th-century method of trying to calculate brain size by filling the skulls of dead humans with seed or lead shot, as Samuel Morton did (see Chapter 2), now it is possible to directly measure living human brains in various ways. Instead of making assumptions about how physiological measures might relate to intelligence, as Morton did, this is now able to be empirically tested. Over the decades since the 1980s, when brain imaging technologies were first introduced, positron emission tomography (PET) scans, structural magnetic resonance imaging (MRI), and functional MRI (fMRI) have been used more and more in researching the neuroscience of intelligence.

Research which draws upon the use of these technologies has evidenced that brain size, or cranial capacity, is indeed connected with intelligence, as is volume of grey matter in the brain and density of white matter.[2] Measures on all of these are higher in individuals who have higher intelligence. (This was even confirmed in a study in 2017 of 1,812 school children in Saudi Arabia which showed that head circumference was significantly associated with intelligence.[3]) Higher IQ has also been correlated with greater neural efficiency. This means that less cortical activity is needed to learn a new task, and better use is made of the brain's glucose resources so that less energy is consumed during performance.[4]

There is the possibility, with these kinds of developments in the physiological study of intelligence, that in the future intelligence might be able to be measured by analysing a brain scan, or by using a method being researched called chronometrics. This involves measuring the speed of information processing in the brain in units of milliseconds and therefore holds the possibility of creating a ratio scale for measuring intelligence, which has so far been absent.[5] Another alternative way of measuring intelligence in the future might be DNA analysis, although this is highly complex. More will be said about genetics later in this chapter (in the section "A Synthesis of Nature and Nurture").

In the meantime, things have also moved on psychometrically. The early intelligence tests developed in the Age of Idealisation, and criticised in the Age of Devaluation, have by the 21st century been refined (and continue to be refined) to address the criticisms. By now, decades' worth of evidence has accumulated that proves the overall reliability and validity of such tests. There will always be exceptions, but it has been shown that, in general, IQ tests make accurate predictions about what a person's cognitive performance can be expected to be, regardless of variables such as age, race, sex, socioeconomic status,[6] and stereotype threat.[7] The idea that intelligence tests are biased has been declared "scientifically dead".[8]

It is very important, however, to be clear on what the tests are actually measuring. What they are measuring is specifically cognitive ability – general intelligence, or g. They are not measuring a person's non-cognitive, global abilities, nor other factors like emotion, nor social skills or morality.

Some tests – like Raven's Progressive Matrices – avoid any questions that relate to knowledge or vocabulary (in other words, crystallised intelligence, or Gc). Such tests only assess abstract reasoning (fluid intelligence, or Gf) so as to ensure the results are more culture fair. This means the results are not affected by the test-taker's background, level of education, or language proficiency. Raven's Progressive Matrices uses the "matrix reasoning" described in Chapter 2, in which all the test-taker has to do is detect logical patterns in sequences of images (although that would still advantage cultures that are well versed in logical thinking). Other popular tests – like the Weschler Intelligence Scale for Children (WISC), the Weschler Adult Intelligence Scale (WAIS), and the Stanford-Binet Intelligence Scale – have been updated so that they are better suited to diverse test-takers.[9]

However, positive manifold – as identified by Charles Spearman (see Chapter 2) – means that it doesn't seem to matter all that much which test is used, because all of them correlate so highly with each other. This was confirmed in a systematic study that analysed over 460 sets of intelligence test results,[10] and it is one of the most well-replicated research findings in the whole field of psychology.[11] Spearman's phrase "indifference of the indicator"[12] means that the surface content of IQ test items is irrelevant. In other words, it doesn't matter whether a person is being asked to complete a puzzle, identify similarities or differences in pictures, or match symbols together as quickly as they can: all of these tasks require cognitive effort. Any task that requires cognitive effort measures intelligence. In fact, it is so easy to measure intelligence that it is almost difficult *not* to measure it: sometimes people who set out to measure a different construct have ended up creating tests of intelligence.[13]

It is one thing to say that some of the assumptions of the Age of Idealisation, so resisted during the Age of Devaluation, have by the 21st century been evidenced to be correct. But how is this information to be used so as to avoid the calamities of the Age of Idealisation? Also, how can we overcome the antagonism towards the subject of intelligence and the researching of it that became entrenched during the Age of Devaluation?

UNDERTAKING RESEARCH ON INTELLIGENCE ETHICALLY

In addressing the impact of what I am calling the Age of Devaluation on the field of intelligence research, several authors[14] have argued for the need to distinguish between facts that are discoverable through scientific research, and the values that we might associate with such facts. Consider the scientific fact of heliocentrism (that the earth revolves around the sun). Such scientific facts are simply neutral pieces of information, items of data that are not in themselves positive or negative. Sure. But people do have values. People interpret a piece of information as being positive or negative, according to their own values. The discovery that the earth revolves around the sun was forcefully resisted because of meanings that were attached to this and the feelings people had about those meanings. Heliocentrism was seen as threatening because it demoted people's sense of importance as being at the centre of the universe, and many had reasons for not wanting to change that preferred world view.

The researchers who pursue the discovery of scientific facts do have values, and they are affected by personal meanings and feelings. And what drives a researcher to search for one kind of fact rather than another? It is a significant loss to humanity for intelligence research to be shunned, but how can it be ethically done? I think a very instructive example of what is involved can be found in looking again at that early skull-filling research methodology.

At almost the same time that Samuel Morton was carrying out his cranial capacity calculations of five racial groups in the USA, anatomist and physiologist Friedrich Tiedemann was carrying out almost identical calculations in Germany. He measured the cranial capacity of more than 400 skulls, also from five racial groups, and published his findings in 1836 and 1837.[15] The measurements of internal capacity that Tiedemann arrived at matched almost exactly the measurements that Morton arrived at. However, what these two researchers then did with their respective sets of data was entirely different from each other.

Morton calculated the *average* brain weight for each race and then compared and ranked these averages *across* the races. He used these figures to argue that the races lower in the rankings should be subservient to those higher in the rankings. He advocated this as a justification for slavery.

Tiedemann, on the other hand, did not calculate averages of the measurements of each race. What he concentrated on was the fact that the data showed a *range* of brain weights *within* each race. He took the fact that there was a range of brain weights within each race as evidence that all races were equal. He used his findings to proclaim that it was unjustifiable to consider any race superior to any other, and he denounced the slave trade as abhorrent.

This comparison between Morton's and Tiedemann's contrasting methods of analysing and interpreting their data highlights that there are always choices to be made when carrying out research. It also highlights how differently something can be investigated depending on the underlying values and motivations of the researcher. Morton was seeking to endorse racism; Tiedemann was seeking to eliminate it.

A SYNTHESIS OF NATURE AND NURTURE

Methods of investigating the genetic contribution to intelligence have also moved on a lot since the 19th-century claims Francis Galton made (see Chapter 2) about the heritability of intelligence. Heritability is the percentage of variation in a trait, in a population, that is accounted for by genetics. A 21st-century methodology that can directly compare the DNA between any individuals is genome-wide complex trait analysis (GCTA).[16] Findings from GCTA have supported the same trends that were found through earlier research endeavours which relied on the methodology of studying pairs of twins in order to try to establish how heritable intelligence is.

Twin studies compared similarity in intelligence between identical twins, who share all of their DNA, to the similarity in intelligence between non-identical, or fraternal, twins, who only share half of their DNA. These studies found that identical twins have a much higher correlation in IQ (over 0.80) than fraternal twins do (around 0.60).[17] Such studies have also shown that shared home environments, as well as non-shared environments (influences outside of the home), cease having much effect on IQ beyond the age of 18. This is because once children have grown up and have a choice over their own environment, they choose what level of complexity they prefer according to their genetic level of intelligence (a bit like my example in Chapter 1 of people choosing their preferred level of complexity in how they do their shopping). This can sound confusing, but what it means is that heritability of intelligence increases into adulthood, at which point it has over 80% heritability. This makes intelligence one of the most highly heritable of all human characteristics.

Although intelligence is so genetically influenced, it has proven to be not at all easy to try to find which genes relate to intelligence. There has already been identification of genes that are involved, but one thing that has become clear is that intelligence is polygenic. This means that many genes are involved that each have a small effect.[18]

Over the decades, many attempts have been made to increase intelligence through environmental interventions – like the playing of Mozart to young children which was mentioned in Chapter 3. These have either produced no impact on IQ or no significant or lasting impact.[19] An example of a very costly, large-scale, and intensive environmental intervention to try to raise IQ is the early educational programme Head Start, initiated in the USA in the 1960s. This – and others like it – recorded a rise in IQ of only a few points, which then declined again after the intervention ended.[20] This has been termed the "fade-out effect".[21]

Nutritional attempts to increase IQ – such as through breastfeeding and omega-3 supplementation – have produced zealous advertising campaigns but contradictory findings.[22] Other interventions, involving cognitive enhancement drugs and non-invasive brain stimulation using magnetic fields, electric currents, and cold lasers, have had a limited short-term impact on performance but failed to increase IQ.

Even worse, some of these have actually resulted in reduced IQ test performance.[23] Trying out novel interventions carries risks.

Whilst attempts to increase intelligence have often been dubious, along the way there has been discovery of several uncontested facts about what damages intelligence. Where nutrition is concerned, one clear fact that has been found is that a deficiency in iodine dramatically reduces IQ.[24] Anything that harms the structure or functioning of the brain will lower IQ. This includes head injuries, certain diseases, environmental toxins, and substance use. Proven barriers to foetal and childhood intellectual development include maternal alcohol consumption during pregnancy, prolonged malnutrition, and exposure to lead in the atmosphere.[25] Higher birth weight is correlated with higher intelligence: mothers with higher IQ tend to have babies with higher birth weight, and babies with higher birth weight tend to develop higher IQ. So, you might wonder, is it the birth weight that is making a difference, or the mother's IQ that is making a difference?

This introduces another important issue in intelligence research. It can be hard to distinguish what is heritable from what is environmentally affected. For example, research has shown that people with higher socioeconomic status (often abbreviated to SES) tend to have higher IQ. This is often interpreted as meaning that higher income and better lifestyles *produce* higher intelligence – in other words, that it is a nurture effect. However, by the 21st century we have a weight of research evidence that suggests it is the other way around – more of a nature effect.[26] According to such research, when children who live in families with higher socioeconomic status are found to have higher IQ, such children have benefitted more from the intelligence that they have genetically inherited from their parents than they have from the privileged lifestyles that their homes are providing for them: it is the *intelligence* that produces the better lifestyle, not the better lifestyle that produces the intelligence.

This makes sense given the findings that both the shared and non-shared environments of children cease having much effect on IQ by adulthood. However, research has also shown that people with higher

IQ tend to choose to spend a longer time in education, and that a longer time spent in education generally produces higher income.[27] Having a higher income then, of course, facilitates a better lifestyle. It can be seen from this how intelligence can lead to better lifestyles. However, it is not as simple as that.

The kind of occupation, income, and lifestyle that a person achieves is also strongly influenced by what is socially transmitted. And the presence (or absence) of wealth determines what social opportunities are accessible, so that self-perpetuating cycles get generated. For example, schools like the famous Eton College (mentioned in Chapter 2) have astoundingly high fees that have to be able to be afforded by the families of the vast majority of the pupils who attend – financial assistance is only made available to a small percentage of pupils. The wealth and "branding" of the school foster a culture of self-confidence. The social contacts made there provide pupils with early familiarity with and access to routes of power and influence. For example, at various intervals over the decades, those who attended Eton would find themselves sharing a classroom with members of the British Royal Family, as it has long been that pre-eminently privileged family's preferred school for educating its sons. The British Royal Family is near the apex of a centuries-long social order, with all the attendant opportunities that accompany the holding of such a position in society.

There can be long-term benefits to children who are exposed to these kinds of social and financial advantages. These can, for example, smooth the way for such pupils to confidently take up positions of leadership in the world – no less than 20 UK prime ministers were educated at Eton. This can be achieved even if their level of intelligence is lower than that of others who have not had those advantages and therefore do not have the confidence or social networks that promote leadership. (UK Prime Minister Boris Johnson, who attended Eton, did not pass the Mensa admission test that requires an IQ score in the top 2% of the population.)

Given the impact on life outcomes of social advantages or disadvantages, it is significant to look at how these become entangled with – and how they might be separated from – the issue of intelligence. For example, we saw earlier in the chapter how initiatives like the Head Start programme aimed to raise IQ and failed to make any real impact on IQ. However, they did have a positive social impact: they succeeded in breaking cycles of social and behavioural problems for participants and in increasing their rates of entry to college.[28]

Although it has overall proven to be easier for environmental influences to harm intelligence than to enhance it because intelligence is so highly heritable, the environment always has an impact. Intelligence is never 100% heritable. Each person has what has been termed a "reaction range",[29] meaning the range of IQ that could be possible for that person to obtain given his or her genetic composition. The level within that range that the person achieves will depend on the quality of their environment. Genotype refers to a person's genetic make-up, and phenotype relates to how that genetic make-up manifests as a result of interaction between genes and environment. A baby born to very high-IQ parents who then suffers prolonged malnutrition will not be able to reach the full phenotypic expression of his or her genotypic potential. How genes interact with the environment is what is studied in the field of epigenetics, which is extremely complex.

THE THEORY OF INTELLIGENCE THAT HAS BEST STOOD THE TEST OF TIME AND RESEARCH

The one elegantly simple conceptualisation that research findings over the decades have repeatedly reiterated is the presence of a general factor of intelligence that influences performance on all other cognitive tasks – what Charles Spearman originally identified in 1904 as g. Contemporary psychometric theories of intelligence[30] differ in how they see g as relating to other broad abilities and more specific abilities, how many different categories of abilities there are, and in what hierarchical relationship they stand to each other. However, most theories still accept the existence of g, as do most experts.[31]

The existence of a *g* factor has been found across many human cultures and even in nonhuman primates and in dogs and rats.[32] Findings in 21st-century research and neuroscience point to a higher *g* factor as being "a positive indicator of high system integrity".[33] This appears to support Francis Galton's original 19th-century hypothesis that intelligence was a manifestation of the general efficiency of the nervous system.[34]

STABILITY OF INTELLIGENCE OVER TIME

In science, the construct of general intelligence has clearly stayed completely stable over time. In people, individual IQ has been shown to stay generally stable through childhood and into adulthood[35] but starts to decline in older age.[36] Fluid intelligence (Gf) deteriorates more with age than does crystallised intelligence (Gc). Gf is affected by speed of reaction, which decreases with age, whereas Gc accumulates over the years: the knowledge and skills a person has acquired – especially if reinforced repeatedly through regular use – can stay intact into advanced old age unless disrupted by injury or disease. This is evident in, for example, concert pianists who continued to perform well into their 90s (such as Arthur Rubinstein) and even their 100s (in the cases of Alice Sommer-Herz and Draga Matkovic). Such pianists mastered performance repertoires in their youth which they kept impeccable through repeated playing over the decades.

Stability of IQ in whole nations has also been tested. The "Flynn effect" refers to studies by James Flynn which showed a rise in the average IQ scores across many Western nations during the 20th century.[37] However, the opposite has been recorded during the 21st century, termed the "negative Flynn effect".[38] The rise has been attributed largely to the lowest IQ scores in those nations improving through improved foetal and infant nutrition and health.[39] The subsequent reverse of this has been attributed to the gains that could be made in this way having peaked, and what is called the dysgenic impact now becoming apparent, meaning the impact of the fact that people with higher IQ are having fewer, or no, children.[40]

NEURODIVERSITY

The data that have by now accumulated in the 21st century from brain imaging, DNA analysis, and more than 100 years of psychometric evidence are enough to have established conclusively that genetically affected, neurobiologically based differences in intelligence do exist amongst human beings. And this is where I wish to bring in the term "neurodiversity", as this is a term that refers to how our brains (neuro) are widely different from each other (diversity).

Neurodiversity is a term that has mostly been used to refer to atypical ways of neurological functioning, such as are present in dyslexia and autism. It has also been debated whether the term can be applied to other conditions which – like dyslexia and autism – have traditionally been pathologised, such as bipolar disorder. An important concern that has been expressed about the concept of neurodiversity is that it should not be used to downplay the challenges that people with such atypical conditions face and the special supports that they require to help them to manage.

Whilst wishing to hold open an attitude of critical thinking about how the concept of neurodiversity is used, I would still like to argue for differences in levels of intelligence between individuals to go under the banner of neurodiversity. This is because research has shown[41] that variations in levels of intelligence do correspond with differences in brain structure and function. If differences in intelligence were to be publicised and accepted as aspects of neurodiversity, then perhaps these could be more openly identified and discussed and managed. This may help communication about this important aspect of humanity to stop being suppressed and burdened by the stigma of previous eras' baggage. A person has no control whatsoever over what their individual "reaction range" is, and therefore it would be progress for societies to respect and practise compassion for the psychological, social, and economy-related implications of the full spectrum of reaction ranges.

REVISITING EMOTIONAL INTELLIGENCE

According to new research, people might also not always have as much control as was previously thought over how much emotional intelligence they display. We saw in the last chapter how, during the Age of Devaluation, emotional intelligence started to be emphasised and how very high-IQ individuals could be criticised for not seeming to have enough of it, as though it was a situation of their own making. Studies in 2016[42] and 2018[43] have started to establish a link between very high IQ and autism.

Autism is a condition of neuroatypicality – meaning the brain is differently configured in autistic people from the way which tends to be the case in the majority of people. It is characterised by people with autism experiencing difficulty with social imagination, interpretation, interaction, and communication. Autism has typically been associated with low IQ, and it is often masked in those with high IQ because they use their other abilities to compensate for it. However, individuals with autism are experienced by neurotypical others as being "different", and they do struggle in social situations (including in developing friendships and workplace and romantic relationships). In an Age of Integration, such individuals could have their quality of life improved enormously – and the contribution they are able to make to society enhanced – if general understanding about autism increases and more support for it is made available.

HOW THE AGE OF INTEGRATION HAS BEGUN

It could be considered that the scene has been well set for an era of synthesis or integration in relation to intelligence, given that there is already widespread evidence in many areas of Western culture of a growing tolerance of, welcoming of, and engagement with diversity regarding other human characteristics such as race, gender, and sexuality. But intelligence is not (yet) recognised as a core aspect of human diversity.

In the UK, some legislation has been put in place to prevent diversity-related discrimination. For example, the Equality Act 2010 names "protected characteristics" against which it is prohibited to discriminate in various spheres of life such as work, education, and public sector services.[44] The named protected characteristics are: age, disability, gender reassignment, marriage and civil partnership, race, religion or belief, sex, and sexual orientation. Intelligence is not named. Within this law, "disability" is defined as "physical or mental impairment". That means that it protects very low intelligence as a disability. Very high intelligence, however, remains unrecognised as an individual difference that has daily life implications for affected persons. We have seen in preceding chapters how much the characteristic of intelligence permeates human experience and activity, how it has underpinned majorly impactful social policies, and how it is scientifically correlated with so many life outcomes. It could therefore be said that it is an omission that intelligence is not a human characteristic that is recognised in law.

Another area where there has been a growing encouragement of greater diversity is in the workplace. In 2018, global management consultancy McKinsey & Company published a report – *Delivering through Diversity*[45] – which makes a strong case for inclusion and diversity in corporations, the public sector, and third-sector organisations worldwide. Their research on over 1,000 companies in 12 countries established a direct link between a more diverse composition of staff and leadership roles and a higher financial performance of the company. However, they define diversity mainly in terms of gender, ethnicity, and culture, with some mention of socioeconomic status and sexual orientation. Again, there is no mention of intelligence or of neurodiversity. Addressing this could be very helpful, as it is well-documented that individuals with very high IQ are often not understood and not catered for in workplaces, leading to conflict, high rates of job turnover, and underemployment of ability.[46] I would argue that neurodiversity needs to be added as a dimension to legal and organisational diversity frameworks.

We have looked at how language has evolved over the ages, particularly in relation to how intellectual disability has been referred to

(Chapter 2). There are signs of a 21st-century evolution of language in relation to intellectual agility. I mentioned in the previous chapter how words like "nerd" and "geek" would be used to taunt high-IQ individuals during the Age of Devaluation. This has also been reflected in other publications. For example:

"Geek!" "Nerd!" "Freak!" "Brainiac!" Stereotyping. Ostracizing. Distancing. "I'm not like everyone else. I'm not acceptable. There's something wrong with me". From preschool on, gifted children often feel flawed.[47]

A news feature on the Mensa website explains how Potential Plus UK (formerly the National Association for Gifted Children) joined forces with Kidscape, Carers Trust, Diversity Role Models, and the Autistic Society on a project called Being Me to support children who are bullied at school for "being different".[48] It cites particle physicist Jeff Forshaw as saying in support of this project:

Labelled as "geeks", "clever clogs", "teacher's pet", "swot" or worse, being bullied can make the lives of these children with high learning potential absolutely miserable.

Many of my very high-IQ clients and research interviewees reported to me the suffering they had experienced from this kind of abuse. However, I found myself in an unexpected media storm in December 2019 following having been reported to have said that laws that protect other minority groups against discrimination should be extended to protect high-IQ individuals from being harassed with such insults. Media outlets around the world picked this up, and the main public reaction was to say it was completely ridiculous because being called a nerd or geek was a "badge of honour" and no longer derogatory. Even the hair and make-up artists at the ITV television studios in London, who were preparing me very early one morning to go on *Good Morning Britain* to debate the issue, were saying to me, "But our children think it's really cool now to be a nerd or geek".

The contradictions, however, were interesting. I received emails saying "You nerd! You geek! You nerdy geek!" They were clearly trying to insult me, yet they were doing it with words which they were telling me were no longer insulting. The funniest comments were "What the Falck?" and "That Dr Falck should just Falck off". But why, I wondered, if it was so ridiculous, did it draw so much attention? And stir so much anger? It even made the front page of one of the tabloid newspapers, scoffing: "Cry-Baby Nerds Want Jokers Sent to Jail".[49] Now I know what it feels like to get caught live amidst a paradigm shift, where old and new associations to words swirl and clash and an evolved way of respecting something co-exists alongside continuing unchecked prejudices against the same thing.

A book that endorses this paradigm shift is Steve Silberman's (2015) book *Neurotribes*, in which he writes: "The kids formerly ridiculed as nerds and brainiacs have grown up to become the architects of our future".[50] Because publications with this kind of perspective seem to have gathered momentum leading up to, and following, 2015, I am placing 2015 as expressing the beginning of the Age of Integration. This is the year after the turning point of 2014 that was presented in the previous chapter as having marked the shift away from the Age of Devaluation.

Although intelligence is not acknowledged in the kinds of frameworks and laws mentioned previously, it has found acknowledgment in one quintessentially 21st-century way. With the explosion of new expressions of gender and sexuality in this era, a whole sexuality centred on intelligence has been named. If your orientation is to be sexually attracted to someone on the basis of nothing about them except their intelligence, then your sexual orientation is termed "sapiosexual". Did you know that?

THE PSYCHOLOGY UNDERLYING THE AGE OF INTEGRATION

Most of us harbour a desire, in situations of interpersonal conflict or division, to emerge from the exchange with some form of understanding and a sense of mutually recognised harmony. This wish is what underpins the drive toward an integration of opposing worldviews. For example, if you consider a minor dispute between yourself and a friend or colleague, once both parties have vented their anger – giving voice to their aggression – it is natural to start to become aware of its damaging impact. With such awareness, we begin to care about what moves could be made to try to bring about repair. What underlies the drive towards integration, therefore, is the psychology of our wish to transcend conflicts and divisions, to seek understanding, and to achieve harmony.

In child development, this drive arises out of a growing maturity – the capacity to become aware of the impact of our actions, and to want to make amends. It is what paediatrician and psychoanalyst Donald Winnicott termed a "capacity for concern".[51] Becoming concerned about one another replaces simply giving in to criticisms of others and primitive splittings into good (me/us) versus bad (you/them). With growing psychological maturity, we can start to see that there is both good and bad in all individuals, all approaches, and all issues. Instead of being prodded by our guilt at discriminating against one thing (lower intelligence) by discriminating against its opposite (higher intelligence), now we can assess the damage that has been done and make reparation by becoming concerned both about individuals who have low and who have high IQ and not discriminating against either – an enlightened new era of terminating discrimination.

Predating Winnicott, the work of psychoanalyst Melanie Klein conveys the same important insight, although she explains it in odder terminology. Klein outlined two basic positions that any of us can occupy at different times. She named these the "paranoid-schizoid" position, which she saw as a primitive way of approaching the world that makes way during healthy development for a more mature functioning in the form of the "depressive" position. "Schizoid" means splitting things into good versus bad, which then makes us afraid of – or "paranoid" about – what we have designated as bad. Integrating positive and negative aspects into a more complex whole brings on the "depressive" state of mourning the loss of the ideal: there is no perfect person or perfect solution but a need to keep grappling as fairly and authentically as we can with a more sober and complicated reality.

Being able to integrate is what the philosophy of pluralism[52] is about. Pluralism adopts the view that we live in a complex world in which a multitude of personal, political, cultural, linguistic, and social factors give rise to multiple different needs and preferences. It advocates not rejecting diversity but also not merely tolerating it. Instead, what it encourages is an active inviting of diversity – showing an attitude and practice of openness and curiosity that seeks out and welcomes engaging with diversity.

Importantly, being able to take up this stance derives from being in a state where you are yourself feeling safe and secure (recall Bowlby's "secure base", Chapter 2), with sufficient resources for taking care of having your own needs met. American psychologist Abraham Maslow, a pioneer in the so-called human potential movement, created a model depicting a "hierarchy of needs".[53] This demonstrated that unless our own basic needs are met (beginning with food and shelter), we cannot give our attention to other matters. We can only welcome others if we feel reassured that they are not going to be a threat to us.

Having discussed how an Age of Integration has begun, the next chapter will explore what implications may be involved in implementing this kind of approach to intelligence in various applied contexts that are part of our day-to-day lives.

5

APPLIED (HUMAN) INTELLIGENCE

This chapter examines how the phenomenon of human (rather than artificial) intelligence is dealt with in different applied contexts, looking at educational, occupational, medical, and legal settings. These correspond respectively with the special divisions that the field of psychology has in educational psychology, occupational/organisational psychology, clinical psychology, and forensic psychology. I have stipulated that I am referring to human intelligence because a striking sign of the times is that there is currently very much more talk and publication on the applications and implications of AI than of IQ.

I will discuss broadly the current status quo regarding human intelligence in these applied contexts, showing how the three ages portrayed in the preceding chapters relate to these: in other words, where we are now because of where we have been, and where could we go next? Questions will be posed about how practice would be affected if the full spectrum of human intelligence were to be more openly and sensitively acknowledged and responded to in these contexts. What might Age of Integration thinking – an embracing of neurodiversity – look like in each of these different settings?

STARTING WITH TWO CASE STORIES

A work acquaintance tells you that her 9-year-old niece, Rita, is in hospital having an operation. Later in the week, you ask how she is recovering from the surgery. Your co-worker says that, actually, it wasn't an operation, but that they had had to anaesthetise Rita in order to examine her throat. She seemed to have an infection, but although three family members were present with her, they couldn't get her to let the doctors near her. You are baffled that a child of that age could require hospitalisation in order to achieve a routine throat examination.

A friend tells you that she has once again had to take her 91-year-old father, Carl, who has Parkinson's disease, to his neurologist, because his recent change in medication has again been causing very difficult symptoms. There have been several episodes like this over the past couple of years, with the neurologist trying to get the medication right and Carl experiencing various kinds of distressing physical incapacitation, confusion, hallucinations, and falls. Your friend reports that during the appointment this week, the neurologist finally said to her, "Through trial and error I believe I have worked out what is going on. I think Carl is just very sensitive to the medication, and I need to actually give him a much smaller dose than usual". You feel awful for your friend and her father for what they have been going through.

In your reactions to these situations, how likely would it be that you might consider that intelligence had anything to do with what was happening? How ready are professionals to consider this? What are the barriers to this being considered or even talked about?

These are real-life stories (with the names changed). Rita has an intellectual disability. Carl is a member of Mensa, the international high-IQ society. In learning these facts, do you think they are relevant to how the person is behaving or what their needs might be? Something that is apparent from these examples is that there are assumptions about what could be expected of a child of a certain age or about what the correct dose of medication is for a person with a certain condition.

When you hear about Rita's behaviour and the anaesthetic that was needed, it confounds your assumptions about how co-operative a 9-year-old could be expected to be and what resources are required for a throat examination. If you knew that she had an intellectual disability, you would immediately have been able to be understanding and compassionate rather than baffled. But although you have worked with this colleague for several years and she has mentioned her niece a few times, she had never before mentioned that she has an intellectual disability. On this occasion, she at first said that Rita was having an operation. Only later did she tell you what the true situation was. In talking socially about her niece, she was filtering out relevant information that would aid understanding.

With Carl, no-one had ever mentioned to the neurologist that he is a member of Mensa. It might be that even if this had been mentioned, the neurologist would not have seen it as relevant. However, what we (now) know about very high IQ is that it involves neural efficiency and heightened sensitivity (and longevity, so Carl's advanced age – well beyond the average life expectancy for men – is a clue). If the neurologist had been aware of Carl's very high IQ and its relevance, then she might have tried much smaller doses at the outset, and 2 years of suffering could have been prevented for Carl and his loved ones. But individuals with very high IQ are usually well-practiced during social interactions at filtering out any reference to facts or experiences they have that relate to their high IQ.

When Rita's family withhold information about her intellectual disability, they are manifesting the Age of Idealisation's legacy. They are wanting to avoid anticipated discrimination against lower intelligence. When Carl and his family do not disclose his Mensa membership, they are affected by the Age of Devaluation's legacy. They are wanting to avoid anticipated discrimination against higher intelligence. In the Age of Integration, can these attitudes and related fears become a thing of the past? Can intelligence become a human trait that is openly acknowledged, and its relevance taken into account in daily life situations with understanding and compassion and without discrimination? A starting point is that none of us can know about the relevance of this sort of information if we are never taught about intelligence. What is the current status of education regarding intelligence?

THE TEACHING OF (HUMAN) INTELLIGENCE

As described in Chapter 3, during the Age of Devaluation universities became reluctant to teach intelligence as a subject, and even the presence of content on intelligence in textbooks reduced in volume and prominence. What content remains was analysed in a study conducted in 2018.[1] The study examined 29 of what it called the USA's most popular introductory psychology textbooks. It found that the majority of them (79%) contained inaccurate statements and logical fallacies regarding intelligence. An example is that the fact that human beings are on average at least 99.5% alike genetically is cited as meaning that there are no real differences between us.[2] Here is a good explanation of why this is a fallacy:

> All domesticated dog breeds differ by only 0.15% of their genes – a much lower level of genetic variation than humans. By the reasoning of [this fallacy], the breed of a dog doesn't matter for its owner's use because such slight genetic differences are trivial. Therefore, poodles can pull Iditarod sleds, and a pug is a great police dog.[3]

The study of textbooks found that there were certain themes in the textbooks. These were: an exaggeration of environmental influences on intelligence, a minimising of the importance of individual differences, and a suggestion that intelligence tests fundamentally disadvantage diverse test-takers. All three of these biases reflect an Age of Devaluation perspective and contradict the weight of scientific evidence that by the 21st century has been well established. What this means is that students who read and are taught from these textbooks will be left with misconceptions about human intelligence and the field of intelligence research. This affects approximately 1.6 million students annually who enrol in introductory psychology courses in the USA.

These misconceptions will be lasting, as introductory psychology students often have no further exposure to the subject of intelligence: in the USA more than 99% of institutions of higher education offer a course in introductory psychology, but fewer than 10% of all psychology departments offer a course on intelligence as part of their undergraduate syllabus.[4] This is because the American Psychological Association (APA) recommended that intelligence should be covered in introductory psychology courses, but this is not required in undergraduate courses.[5] In the UK, psychology courses accredited by the British Psychological Society (BPS) follow the curriculum guidance set out by the Quality Assurance Agency for Higher Education (QAA) in its periodically updated "Subject Benchmark Statement: Psychology".[6] This statement mentions that it is not meant to be prescriptive and that providers can vary in how they implement it. It includes intelligence as a subject under the category of "individual differences". I have spoken with providers who have interpreted from this that all that needs to be taught about intelligence is intelligence testing, and they cover this by giving only one lecture on intelligence in each psychology course.

In psychology education, therefore, there is very little attention given to intelligence. Yet intelligence is the construct in the whole of psychology that is most highly predictive of human trajectories in many areas, such as in academic achievement, industrial and professional competence, and military performance.[7] In this respect, its neglect makes no sense. But it makes sense in terms of it being a legacy of the damage done by the Age of Idealisation, followed by the reaction against that during the Age of Devaluation. In the Age of Integration, this could usefully be addressed. The APA named five pillars that should be the foundation of any introductory course in psychology. These are: biological, cognitive, development, social and personality, and mental and physical health.[8] They placed intelligence within "social and personality". However, hopefully it is clear from the content of this book so far that intelligence spans all of these areas, either affecting or being affected by each one.

I would like to see the subject of intelligence being engaged with in a more psychosocial and relational way. This means that instead of seeing and teaching it as some curious collection of facts and scientific findings with a horrible history, seeing it as something that we all are affected by and have feelings about and reactions to with regard to ourselves and in relation to each other. This can be done by providing opportunities for experiential engagement with the subject. This means, for example, inviting students to reflect on and discuss questions such as the following sample questions:

> Can you think of a memorable experience you have had of noticing that someone else seemed to have a very different level of ability (higher or lower) compared with your own? In what circumstances did this become apparent? What thoughts and feelings did this stir in you about that person? What thoughts and feelings did this stir in you about yourself? After you noticed this, did it change the way you behaved towards that person? How?[9]

Using such an approach would introduce a way of teaching individual differences differently. When students link concepts with their own experience, they become more actively involved in their learning and more able to apply that learning in their daily lives. If we would like to see the development of Age of Integration thinking and practice in relation to human intelligence in society in general, then a great starting place for this would be to help students to apply it in their own personal thinking and interpersonal reactions.

INTELLIGENCE IN OTHER EDUCATIONAL SETTINGS: SCHOOLS

It was for an educational setting that the first intelligence tests were devised: Alfred Binet's 1904 tests resulted from the French education ministry asking him to find a way of identifying children who were not coping in the school system so that resources could be provided to cater to their different needs. It has remained true ever since, because of the basic fact of individual differences, that any system that tries to uniformly address a collection of mixed human beings will not be suitable for every individual within that group. This is the case in every school in every country where educating a group of diverse learners collectively is attempted. And, as in 1904, it is those who are coping less well who are usually – and often exclusively – the focus for additional resources.

In the UK there is government policy related to Special Educational Needs and Disability (SEND), which makes provision for intellectual disability but not for intellectual agility. When I asked Potential Plus UK, an independent charity supporting young people with high learning potential, what the current policy is on how the needs of the highest IQ children are to be addressed in schools, this was their answer:[10]

> The short answer to current policy status in England is that there is no policy. Ofsted's Education Inspection Framework that was effective from September 2019 does not mention "Most Able" at all in the Schools Handbook (down from 12 mentions in the previous framework). When asked about this they said that this is because teachers should be catering for all groups and that the framework therefore doesn't go into detail about the groups. Except that it does specifically mention SEND (probably because this is statutory) and Disadvantaged (probably because there is funding for this). In late 2017, the then Secretary of State for Education, Justine Greening, announced a Future Talent Fund of £23 million [28m USD] to be used to find out what works for disadvantaged most able learners. This was later reduced to £18m [22m USD] and then cancelled altogether.

To make it clear how different the intellectual functioning is of someone with an IQ at the 98th percentile or higher, a study showed that such students could "assimilate a year's high school course work in about three weeks of intensive study".[11] Imagine the stultifying boredom for someone of that capability when they are forced to spend a whole year on something they could learn in less than a month.

By setting learning curricula, schools are deciding which educational goals should be achieved and by which chronological age. That is their organisational mission. Individuals who are not achieving those goals understandably attract special attention, as they are hindering the organisational mission. Children who are easily surpassing those goals typically do not attract special resources to address their needs because they constitute no problem for the school's achievement of its organisational mission (unless such children become notably disruptive or noncompliant). Very high-IQ children often languish at school, disengaged and underachieving, or are removed from the system by themselves dropping out of school or by their parents taking them out and homeschooling them instead.[12]

Any institution that provides collective education is faced with a basic choice between whether gaining entry to that institution will be selective (candidates selected for admission according to their assessed academic performance) or non-selective. And within each of those options, there will still be the question of how to deal with intellectual differences – for example, to stream or not to stream? (Streaming means dividing groups of students who are taking a particular subject into subgroups according to their performance in that subject.) In many places there is an Age of Devaluation resistance against selection or streaming because of its Age of Idealisation-related negative associations. In all of these options there are two main issues.

The first issue is that of the benefits of diversity versus the benefits of similarity. The world contains a great diversity of intellectual ability, and a child who is in a school that is academically non-selective will be exposed to a "real-world" range of abilities. It could be said that learning how to mix and work with and find your own personal way in relation to intellectually diverse others is important preparation for functioning in the "real world". However, within that "real world" there are also very many subsections of industry and society that are arranged around specific levels of ability. For example, there are very different intellectual requirements for joining a company of lawyers than for joining a company of domestic cleaners, because of the different intellectual demands of those different occupations. It could therefore be argued that educational environments that selectively group together learners who have a similarity in ability are also preparing those learners to function in the "real world", equipping them to do well in the subsection for which they are best suited.

Matching tasks with ability can bring about contentment through individuals neither having to struggle with demands being placed upon them that are demoralisingly too complex for them, nor having to experience the boredom and frustration of being presented only with tasks that are too simplistic to be stimulating and challenging. When individuals feel secure and their personal needs are being satisfied, this provides for them a stable foundation from which generosity is possible towards others, because the demands or needs of others are then not experienced as a threat to their own well-being.

This issue of selective versus non-selective education becomes contentious when one or the other is decided at a governmental level and then imposed on a nation. The Age of Idealisation imposed selective educational models, and the Age of Devaluation imposed non-selective ones. An Age of Integration could promote a variety of provision, freedom of choice as to which kind individuals prefer, and free movement between different kinds so that there is no proscription around this that can cause bitterness, stigma about groupings, and cases of misgroupings that cannot be reversed.

The second issue that comes up in relation to any ability-related groupings that might be made in educational settings is how the psychosocial (psychological and social) aspects of this are managed. A main problem in any selection process, whether selective entry to schools or streaming within schools, is how people feel about this and behave in relation to it. The Age of Idealisation unhelpfully caused associations of superiority to be linked with individuals who are placed in a higher academic band. This problematic discrimination would also cause those in lower academic bands to be linked with associations of inferiority. (One author criticises providing enrichment opportunities for gifted students because it leaves out the rest as "ungifted".[13])

In the Age of Idealisation, attitudes and practices that favoured those with higher ability were promoted uncritically (see the examples in Chapter 2). In the Age of Devaluation, this was reversed. This meant that perceptions around differential ability were not reinvented; all that happened was that schools started to cater more to those whom the Age of Idealisation had discriminated against by instead discriminating against those whom the Age of Idealisation had favoured. I see the Age of Integration as being about a considered reinvention of this, not pretending we are all the same – realistically acknowledging the differences – but ending the previous eras' ways of discriminating against the differences. Ending such discrimination would involve being thoughtful about and carefully intervening in three main areas: educational practices, language, and playground behaviour.

With regard to educational practices: within any model of collective education, one cannot get away from the necessity of having to plan what the curriculum is going to be that will be taught. Current SEND provision already caters to those at the lower end of the spectrum of intelligence, and there is clearly a need for such provision to be continued. However, in order to make provision for the neglected higher end of that spectrum who are rarely catered for, two fairly simple adjustments are possible. The first is to make the next level of the set curriculum available to the most able learners. The second is to allow such learners more autonomy in their learning. These are proven adaptations.[14] (An imaginative example of another kind of adaptation was told to me by Rebecca Howell, Senior Education Consultant for Potential Plus UK, as we chatted at their offices in the Mansion at Bletchley Park. Bletchley Park is famous for being the place where Alan Turing and other cryptanalysts broke enemy ciphers for Britain during World War Two. Howell said that very able learners could be kept engaged by having their school tasks presented to them in code.)

In terms of language, one cannot get away from the fact that achieving excellence will (typically) be seen, and spoken of, as being positive. However, recalling what we have looked at regarding typical psychological processes of splitting, it would be helpful to develop caution about using labels of "good" versus "bad" and to be thoughtful about how praise is given. If we find ourselves disappointed or frustrated because someone has achieved less than what was expected, we could consider whether there might be an intellectual disability involved. If we find ourselves very impressed because someone has achieved much more than was expected, it could be helpful to remember that for those with intellectual agility it will be easy for them to far exceed average goals, and that when it has been so easy for them they will not personally view it as an achievement. If we *change* our expectations from being fixed on the average, then we can take it as normal that there will be some who will naturally exceed average goals, and so greet this as less of a surprising anomaly and more as something to be expected and then responded to appropriately when it manifests.

Concerning playground behaviour: children easily fall into splitting – treating each other as though they are "good" or "bad", idealising those who excel, devaluing those who struggle, and taunting any who stand out for either of those reasons. If we are alert to such behaviours, then when they are seen we could helpfully intervene to teach a positive embracing of neurodiversity. Children can also be helped to understand that there is a greater complexity of qualities that is integrated in each person, moving beyond simplistic views and judgments of "good" versus "bad".

How children are taught about and helped to understand these issues grows out of how intelligence is understood and taught about in our society in general. How are the teachers and parents who are raising and educating these children perceiving intelligence and feeling about intelligence themselves? Just as we have been looking previously at intelligence being taught about in university courses, it might be helpful to teach about it and acknowledge it more openly

and compassionately within schools also. It can be explained as neurodiversity, together with other kinds of human diversity that already
form a standard part of the curriculum in personal, social, health, and
economic (PSHE) education.

INTELLIGENCE IN OCCUPATIONAL SETTINGS

A study of organisational psychology textbooks showed that these
devoted an average of just under four paragraphs to the subject of
cognitive intelligence, even though IQ has been proven to be one
of the most powerful predictors of job performance, especially in
more complex jobs.[15] There was about double the space – and more
accurate information – for the topic of emotional intelligence, even
though scientific research has not generated the same evidence for
the predictive importance of emotional intelligence as for cognitive
intelligence.[16] This is clearly an Age of Devaluation bias, in reaction
against the Age of Idealisation's emphasis on IQ. An Age of Integration would involve encouraging recognition of the important part
that neurodiversity plays in preparation for a job, candidate selection
for jobs, and how workers react to one another once they are in a
job. And it would require a change in how different sorts of jobs are
valued.

Some kind of preparation for a job – in terms of education and/
or training – is a prerequisite in most occupations. Where the job
is complex, such as being a surgeon or an astronaut, many years of
preparation are needed. Education and training are costly to provide,
and how do you know that it is a suitable investment, that the person
being trained will go on to work in that job? This is where assessment methods help. And although such assessments are not said to
be measuring intelligence, they are very similar to IQ tests. Different
cognitive abilities are clearly emphasised in different jobs – a barris-
ter needs strong verbal ability, an actuary requires high mathematical
proficiency, a pilot has to have reliable spatial competence. And it is
these kinds of abilities that such tests measure.

How do you find the right person for the job? In recruitment, these kinds of assessments are again very helpful for candidate selection, for the same reasons. They allow anyone to apply for a job and can guide employers to make the best match between applicant and job requirements. This is particularly necessary in situations where very large numbers of applicants and job roles are involved, such as the tens of thousands of different positions that need to be filled for a country to create an effective military.

Once people are in jobs, an Age of Integration would involve having resources and strategies available that support neurodiverse workers to function at their best in the workplace. Understanding about neurodiversity can help everyone accept their own individual differences without shame, low self-esteem, or arrogance and accept others' individual differences without expectations that are too low or too high. This would involve sharing information about different bands in the human intelligence spectrum, how they manifest, and how they differ from each other within a culture of valuing all bands. Human resources (HR) staff who are trained in this could nurture such a culture, and coaches could be used to support its implementation, being ready to recognise when issues arise whether they might relate to intellectual differences. Currently intellectual differences are not at all straightforwardly acknowledged as a named category of diversity that is present and influential. Naming it and learning about it can then enable suitable adaptations to be implemented for responding to it.

An important part of addressing the psychosocial aspects of embracing neurodiversity would be the bringing about of a change of the culture in which certain jobs are treated as more valuable than others. All jobs are necessary in a fully functioning economy. It is unavoidable that people will continue to be impressed by jobs in proportion to their complexity, because we naturally admire those who demonstrate the ability to do things that not everyone can do. However, valuing all levels of ability for all the different ways that these can be employed promotes a culture of making all individuals able to feel proud of their personal contribution. And individuals who feel valued and satisfied within their work make a healthier and happier society.

To effect such a change, certain changes of perspective would be necessary. For example, alternative indicators of "success" would need to be developed that move away from the traditional measure of gross domestic product (GDP), because GDP focuses solely on economic growth. Several different alternatives have been put forward and explored. One example is the Happy Planet Index (HPI)[17] which is a calculation based on subjective well-being multiplied by life expectancy and divided by ecological footprint. This recognises that people want to live long and fulfilling lives, and it also recognises the importance of living sustainably within our ecological environment.

INTELLIGENCE IN MEDICAL SETTINGS

In the case examples presented at the start of this chapter, the stories of both Rita and Carl involved input from a medical setting. It is customary that in most medical settings there would be no information available on patients' IQs, unless a person's behaviour had come to attract attention as being suggestive of unusually low IQ. This way of thinking – in which identifying very low IQ is considered relevant but very high IQ is generally dismissed as inconsequential – is what I would term a "mental impairment bias". It is an understandable repercussion of the Age of Devaluation. However, very high IQ is not inconsequential. Research has shown that extremely high IQ ("hyper brain") is associated with various physiological sensitivities ("hyper body").[18] This means that an IQ in the 98th percentile and higher is implicated as a potential risk factor for many physiological conditions that involve elevated sensory, and altered immune and inflammatory, responses. How many doctors know about this and think about this? They might be familiar with low intelligence affecting a patient's capacity to comply with a medication regime, but do they consider that with very high intelligence there might be alteration needed to the typical medication regime that is prescribed because of the exceptional efficiency of the patient's nervous system?

Situations in which IQ is currently specifically thought about in medical settings are those where assessment is required of how a person's cognitive functioning has been affected following having had, for example, a traumatic head injury. Or IQ tests are used in cases of old-age–related cognitive deterioration in conditions such as dementia to assess whether affected individuals are able to take care of their own affairs. Apart from these situations, IQ not generally being thought about as a dimension that has an impact means that people are generally treated in a way that assumes they have an average IQ. This takes care of the majority of the population (see the bell curve explanation in Chapter 2). However, it is unsuitable for those at the bell curve's tails.

A mental impairment bias in medical settings leads to inaccurate interpretations of data. For example, someone with extreme intelligence who has had a stroke is assessed as being fine afterwards, because he easily passes the simple IQ test that is administered. Yet all those around this person are grief-stricken by seeing how much of his prior abilities have been lost.

It is a similar situation where drug abuse and mental illness are concerned, which are often related to each other (and those with highest IQ are at higher risk of both).[19] An example is a case where a psychiatrist told a young man that his few years of drug use and related repeated psychotic breakdowns would have harmed his cognitive functioning. A formal assessment was then done which placed the young man at the 70th percentile IQ. The psychiatrist greeted this as good news, saying, "This means you are the exception: what you have been through has not impaired your cognitive function".

The problem with this is that not having any baseline figures for this young man from previous years meant that the psychiatrist's evaluation was a complete assumption, based on the bell curve. Because 70th percentile is higher than average, the psychiatrist assumed that no harm had been done. However, the young man himself, and those around him, knew that his intellectual capacity had definitely diminished. His pre-breakdown trajectory suggested a 98th-percentile IQ or higher. Yet because there had never been a formal test that set a baseline, there was no objective analysis possible of what had been lost, and the loss was therefore not medically registered or responded to with understanding and compassion as well as appropriate intervention. It also gave the patient the false message that his actions had not been destructive. What would it be like if, in an Age of Integration, IQ became one of the areas of routine information that a patient usually comes with, such as blood type, and if it were treated as pragmatically and neutrally as differences in blood type are treated?

A related area of practice to that of physical health is that of mental health. It has long been recognised that individuals with intellectual disabilities are more likely to develop mental health problems,[20] such as schizophrenia.[21] It is more recent that research has established a correlation between very high IQ and increased risk of certain psychological conditions including attention deficit hyperactivity disorder (ADHD), autism spectrum disorder (ASD), and affective disorders,[22] particularly bipolar disorder.[23] There is generally no provision in psychiatry, psychology, psychotherapy, and counselling training for practitioners to learn about how levels of intelligence relate to mental health. In a typical example, in the book *Counselling and the Life Course*,[24] the author discusses the need, when counselling adolescents, to be aware of how they may need help if they are lagging behind their peers and have to learn to cope with their learning difficulties. No mention is made of those who are far ahead of their peers, who may equally need help in learning to cope with their learning agility.

Knowing a person's IQ can be helpful information that can alert practitioners to what issues might be relevant, and this can aid and speed up diagnosis, yet this is ignored. In *The Practitioner's Handbook – A Guide for Counsellors, Psychotherapists and Counselling Psychologists*,[25] seven important aspects of individual difference are mentioned as being race, gender, sexual orientation, class, disability, religion, and age. There is no mention of intelligence. Although this is a dimension of individual difference that substantially affects our way of engaging with the world, it is not raised in medical or therapy consulting rooms as something salient to consider.

INTELLIGENCE IN LEGAL SETTINGS

In the context of law enforcement within a society, embracing neurodiversity would mean learning about and thinking about how intelligence relates to criminality, and translating that into practice. For example, a disproportionately high number of individuals who are arrested have below-average IQ. It has been argued recently (2018) that students of criminal justice – who have been said to be likely to have above-average IQ – would be better prepared for their work if they were given a chance to encounter individuals with lower levels of intellectual functioning and develop an understanding of what this involves.[26]

Criminal justice systems already recognise very low intelligence as a factor that needs to be considered when assessing what responsibility someone has for a crime they have committed. If a person is not held to be intellectually capable of having responsibility for their crime – that is, it is deemed that they could not have known better – then the person is not put on trial in the same way. IQ tests are used to measure intellectual functioning to determine criminal accountability.

In the UK, having an IQ score of 70 or lower – which is the range defined as constituting intellectual disability – makes a person eligible for what is termed criminal justice liaison and diversion.[27] This means that communication and co-operation are undertaken amongst different services to divert such offenders away from courts and prisons and into other services instead. Appropriate alternative services could relate to health treatment or social care and support services.

The emphasis of this is on early detection and intervention. This means detainees being screened at the police arrest stage. To implement this, police need to have awareness of intellectual disability. It has been recommended[28] that such awareness should be a key component in training programmes for staff throughout the criminal justice system, including the police, probation officers, and the judiciary. In these recommendations, however, there is once again no mention of . . . by now you'll have guessed it . . . intellectual agility, or very high IQ.

It is true that many studies have established that increased intelligence is directly correlated with decreased criminality. However, it is rarely quoted, and clearly far less known about, that this relationship changes at the very highest IQ levels. At the 98th percentile and higher, criminality rises. (In Chapter 1, we saw high-IQ Frank Morris's ingenious escape from Alcatraz as an example of the accomplishments of extreme intelligence.)

Understanding more about the reasons for this is important. It is a manifestation of the principle of "parallels at the extremes"[29] of the bell curve of intelligence. What this means is that individuals at the lowest, and the highest, extremes of human intelligence can experience similar kinds of problems in terms of not fitting in with a world that is designed for those of average intelligence.

In criminology, the dominant theory of what causes delinquency is American sociologist Travis Hirschi's social bond theory.[30] It shows how criminal behaviour is fostered by a weakening of the following four social elements: attachment (close relationships with others); commitment (valuing systems of social conformity); belief (believing in conventional social norms); and involvement (being engaged and absorbed in non-offending activities). Both very low- and very high-IQ individuals stand out as being different from the average-IQ majority. They accordingly experience more difficulty gaining social acceptance and forming close relationships (weak attachment). They will not value social systems such as schools (weak commitment), as these are designed to cater best to the average and are not suitable in the same way for individuals at either end of the extremes of intelligence. Becoming disillusioned with the normal routines of life that are not well designed for their atypical ways of functioning, such individuals lose faith in the point of such routines (weak belief). Not being interested in the typical activities that interest average-IQ people (weak involvement), they will look for alternative ways to use their time, and, given their disillusionment, these may include offending activities. Such risks are recognised in the alternative supports and services that are offered to offenders with very low IQ. But what about those with very high IQ?

Very high-IQ individuals typically go through a school system that ignores them and fails them, where they do not have their intellectual needs met. This leads to bitterness, boredom, feeling like a social misfit, and having no channel for prosocially using their high ability. Could very high IQ therefore be an excuse for having committed a crime because the offender was so bored and his or her needs so neglected?

Police and other related professionals should surely be similarly educated in the implications and identification of very high IQ. In a criminal justice system that fully embraced neurodiversity, would the appropriately compassionate and prosocial recourse be that liaison and diversion are similarly employed in cases where the offender involved is tested and reveals an extremely high IQ? Legendary fraudster Frank Abagnale – who managed to pose as an airline pilot, doctor, and lawyer, and drew millions of dollars using forged cheques[31] – spent time in prison in France and Sweden. After serving 4 years of a 12-year sentence in the USA, a deal was done to have him swap his jail sentence for service to the FBI on their anti-fraud squad. Who better to know how the mind of a fraudster works? Having someone with Abagnale's criminal expertise on their side, rather than wasting away behind bars, was an eminently intelligent move. Could more such deals be done?

In this chapter we have started to explore broadly what an embracing of neurodiversity might look like in each of four different applied contexts. In the previous chapters we looked at the psychology underlying the different approaches there have been to human intelligence over the ages. In order for any innovative new ways of thinking and practice about intelligence to be implemented in a developing Age of Integration, the underlying psychology will always first need to be understood and tackled. That is the focus of the next and concluding chapter.

IN CONCLUSION
Which approach do you choose?

A recent article in the journal *Intelligence* referred to the "mismatch between scholarly consensus on intelligence and the beliefs of the general public".[1] I hope this book has helped tackle that mismatch by charting how we have arrived at such a situation and showing how psychological factors have complicated the building and sharing of scientific knowledge about human intelligence. There are identifiable psychological motivations and reactions that have given rise to Western society's way of approaching human intelligence over the ages, bringing us to where we are now.

We can study the history covered in the previous pages and debate the related issues and social changes on a national and international scale, but it is at an individual level that the beliefs we hold about intelligence influence our behaviour and decisions as we interact with each other in the course of our ordinary day-to-day activities. Learning about the history and the underlying psychology of intelligence gives us the opportunity to be aware of the active role that each of us can play in choosing what approach we personally take towards intelligence. This concluding chapter consolidates the main points of the book and considers how we can implement its insights as we go about our daily lives.

APPROACHES TO INTELLIGENCE OVER THE AGES

The two main ages we have seen in Western society's way of approaching human intelligence have both proven problematic. The Age of Idealisation, pre–World War Two, emphasised nature over nurture and culminated in eugenics. The main problem with the Age of Idealisation thesis is that it is inhumane, discriminating against those with lower intelligence and idealising those with higher intelligence. It does not place equal value on non-cognitive strengths or support individuals who do not perform well in traditional academics to develop in the best way they can. Because of this, people who actually have high intelligence but also have dyslexia, for example, or autism and/or other atypicalities – termed twice exceptionality or dual and multiple exceptionality – remain unidentified and are neglected.

The Age of Devaluation, post–World War Two, emphasised nurture over nature, culminating in the expertise antithesis. The main problem with this is that it is false. It does not face the reality of innate individual differences in intellect. Also, it creates a culture of anti-intellectualism that allows those with very high intelligence to be discriminated against with impunity. They are not recognised and understood, and they are not supported to develop in the best way they can.

Since about 2015, we appear to have started entering an Age of Integration, in which there is a synthesis between nature and nurture, a more sober and educated recognition of the respective influences that both genetic and environmental elements have on intelligence. Integration forges the most humane and realistic path forward for the future, acknowledging individual differences in intelligence but not practicing discrimination in relation to these. I have argued for a straightforward and non-discriminatory acknowledgment and acceptance of intelligence as being simply one of the many aspects of human diversity, an aspect that is part of neurodiversity.

OVERCOMING THE MENTAL IMPAIRMENT BIAS

It is clear from the bell curve of human intelligence (see Chapter 2) that a large majority of people have a similar level of intellectual functioning. Society is, very logically, therefore, predominantly geared towards what is wanted and needed by, and what works for, that majority of the population. Systems, and assumptions, in daily life, in all settings – for example, educational, occupational, medical, and legal – are based on what is expected of and is suitable for that majority of the population. It is when people differ much more markedly from the average that they defy our customary expectations and the ordinary systems are not suitable for them. This applies to individuals who have an IQ score of lower than 70 or higher than 130. These scores are at the two opposite extreme ends of the bell curve.

We have seen that there are parallels at these extremes in terms of the implications for such individuals of not fitting in with the norms of society, whether it is because their intellectual functioning is very much lower, or very much higher, than average. What we have also seen is that society has largely become more aware of and tolerant of intellectual disability and has made adaptations to make provision for this in many areas of life, but that this is not the case with regard to intellectual agility. This mental impairment bias acknowledges that there are special needs connected with having very low intelligence but not with having very high intelligence. It is understandable that contemporary life is skewed towards this Age of Devaluation stance, as that has been the most recent age in Western society's approach towards intelligence. There is room for improvement universally in remembering and being sensitive and responsive to these parallels at the extremes.

CHOOSING OUR APPROACH TOWARDS INTELLIGENCE IN OUR DAILY LIVES

We have seen how the Age of Idealisation and Age of Devaluation have caused intelligence to become a controversialised and neglected subject. We saw in the previous chapter how things might have been different for Carl and his loved ones, and how those around Rita could have better understood her situation, if intelligence had been something that was openly acknowledged and spoken about with accurate information and compassion and without discrimination. And how might things have been different for Ida (from Chapter 1) if intelligence had been approached in a different way?

When Ida ran away from school regularly, her teacher interpreted this as meaning she was a "social drop-out". He did not separate her social disadvantages from her individual make-up. He associated chaotic and noncompliant behaviour with a lack of intelligence and therefore not only failed to nurture her love of biology but even discouraged her from bothering with it. His prejudices blinded him to her potential. I would see it as a positive development if teachers, students, and parents had better education about intelligence, so that people like my supervisee (in the introduction to the book) wouldn't have to feel self-conscious about intelligence and people like Ida wouldn't have to feel afraid of it.

If we notice how we are viewing ourselves and others in relation to intelligence, we can choose what to do about this. Maybe you are an Ida, or a Rita, or a Carl. Or maybe you are raising one, married to one, friends with one, or teaching or working with one. That is why your approach to intelligence matters. It is in our daily thinking and behaviours that we can usefully start to become aware of which age's approach we are being influenced by.

I think about my own approach to intelligence daily. For example, I received an email from a student asking to meet with me to get feedback about how he could improve the essay he had recently handed in. I looked up the essay on our digital system to see what he was referring to. I found that the essay had been graded with a distinction. I noticed myself having an immediate reaction of disbelief – why, when he had already achieved the top grade band, was he asking about how to improve? No sooner had I caught myself having that reaction than I realised how that was a reaction that belonged with Age of Devaluation thinking, in which only those who are struggling are given attention for how to improve. I am in theory a staunch proponent of an Age of Integration ethos, believing that students across all grade bands deserve equal support to keep improving, and yet, in practice, I had a knee-jerk reaction of thinking, "How unnecessary" when I realised this student wanted input on an essay after he had already received a distinction for it. This goes to show how, in spite of our best intentions, we can easily reflect internalised prejudices from previous ages' approaches to intelligence. We need to recognise and tackle these if we want to make changes.

We can start to notice the different ages' ways of thinking in things that we hear and see and read. For example, I recently read a research article on whether all levels of IQ contribute equally to economic growth and technological progress.[2] The conclusion was that those with highest IQ contributed the most. I immediately realised how this is a finding that can easily trigger Age of Idealisation thinking, along the lines of viewing those with higher IQ as being of the most value because they contribute the most to endeavours (economic growth and technological progress) that are currently so widely assumed to be important and desirable. However, an antidote to such thinking is to maintain a holistic – including ecological – perspective. The information from that article may be useful for purposes that are specifically related to economic growth and technological progress. But we may also recognise the limits of the value of – and the difficulties with – economic growth and technological progress.

INCLUSION

A fully functioning economy holds a multitude of different roles that need to be filled, which carry with them various different levels of intellectual challenge. In 21st-century living, fair assessment is necessary of diverse individuals with their diverse needs towards best fulfilling diverse purposes in society. If all levels of intellectual ability are recognised and equally well supported to thrive, with individuals being matched with well-suited roles and all contributions across all roles being well valued, then this can play an important part in improving efficiency and well-being across human populations. When individuals feel secure, with their own needs met, they are able to be open and generous towards others.

In whatever walks of life, and with whatever methods, assessment of ability might be undertaken, if we want to shake previous ages' negative associations to that kind of assessment, then the psychosocial aspects of it will need to be recognised and worked with. People have a tendency to split into "good" versus "bad". For assessment to be something constructive and not divisive, there would need to be careful attention to attitudes and language to help us move beyond reactions that idealise or devalue.

"Intelligent intelligence testing"[3] involves recognising the usefulness of tests but also recognising their limitations, not over-generalising their results, and not seeing the results as "set in stone". Carol Dweck has demonstrated the importance of holding a "growth mindset" rather than a "fixed mindset" in relation to intelligence,[4] so as to encourage individual effort and development and not believe one's life path is determined by any one assessment alone. However, growth is also not unlimited – there is a DNA base that yields a "reaction range" (see Chapter 4). IQ scores can give a sense of a person's reaction range, particularly when this falls within either extreme of the bell curve. For example, we have seen in the previous pages that very high IQ is associated with difficulties in general educational systems, longer life expectancy, a particular crime-risk profile, heightened physiological and psychological sensitivity, and higher susceptibility to certain physical and psychological conditions. Identifying very high IQ could therefore prove useful in helping to identify risk and to provide accurate diagnoses and provision in educational, occupational, medical, and legal settings. If a growth mindset can be maintained, and if it were possible for fear of discrimination to become a thing of the past, then IQ scores could contribute useful baseline information.

When it comes to what to do with data on individual differences such as IQ scores, I think Tiedemann's approach holds an important key for unlocking an Age of Integration. Recall the alternative ways that Morton and Tiedemann handled the data sets that each of them respectively gathered when measuring human skulls (see Chapter 4). What we can do with data sets from IQ tests is not compare averages across different populations. That is the Morton approach. By using Tiedemann's approach, we can recognise that there is a range of different IQ scores in any group of humans no matter on what basis any kind of group division may be created.

The creating of group divisions is increasingly difficult to justify, given that 21st-century life involves so much cross-national, cross-racial, cross-class, and cross-gender intersectionality. It follows that discrete categories no longer apply in the same sort of way that they previously might have. By following Tiedemann's example, we can nurture greater inclusivity, evolving away from group differences thinking in the field of intelligence (or any field). Instead of the divisive practice of separating sections of humanity off into subgroups, can we see ourselves as a group of human beings as a whole, and concentrate on how to respond best to the full range of diversity that is found within that whole human group?

Research (see Chapter 4) has shown us that organisations that incorporate greater human diversity are more successful. Yet we have also seen that in the various current frameworks and legislations concerning diversity, there is no mention of intelligence as a fundamental – and very influential – aspect of human diversity. An inclusion of neurodiversity in all such frameworks would be a valuable way of promoting an Age of Integration in relation to human intelligence.

An increasing of diversity will not, however, work simply by throwing together a collection of diverse individuals. Once they are put together, they have to be able to relate effectively to each other. Unless there is support for achieving inclusion, to generate a sense of safety and acceptance and belonging together in spite of the differences, people will easily fall prey to in-group/out-group discriminatory behaviours. This is because of the psychological principles of safety being paired with similarity and difference with danger.

SAFETY AND SIMILARITY, DIFFERENCE AND DANGER

As human beings we are genetically programmed to seek safety right from infancy onwards through building secure relationships with our significant caregivers. We also secure our safety through seeking to belong with a group of others with whom we can work together to ensure we have the resources and protection needed for survival. A key component in forming relationships and groups is that of seeking similarity with others. This love of similarity – termed "homophily"[5] – underpins our sense of safety with others: we feel that we know what to expect of others when they are similar to ourselves, we feel we can trust them, and when we are with them – our in-group – we feel in a comfort zone. Hostilities arise out of differences: in ancestral life, and in contemporary life, danger is associated with difference. Those whom we do not feel we belong with are characterised as somehow different from us, and they become the out-group.

Cognitive capability – as one of the core areas of our daily functioning – is one of the areas in which we seek similarity with others. We have seen (in Chapter 1) how the principle of compatibility in intelligence forms an important aspect of how we choose friends, lovers, employees, and business leaders. Where there are large differences in intelligence between people, we need education and effort to enable us to understand what is involved and to mediate our homophilic tendencies so that we do not – in our drive to secure safety and avert danger – automatically reject what is different.

MIND THE GAP

When we encounter a clear gap in intellectual functioning between ourselves and someone else, we are presented with the opportunity of choosing how we would like to react to this. For example, if we perceive someone as being brilliant, do we find ourselves feeling threatened? Is there any actual threat involved? Can we be alert to the risk of *Schadenfreude*, of being tempted to act subtly (or worse) to spoil something for that person? Can we counteract that and deliberately try to be compassionate towards that person, recognising that it is so much easier to have compassion for people whom we see as being in some way worse off than ourselves?

Even if we do not feel any threat of danger, we can simply find an encounter with a large intellectual gap troublesome. We have looked, specifically in Chapter 5, at different contexts in which different levels of IQ might be encountered and what the implications might be. It can be helpful to pay attention to this in our day-to-day lives – mind the gap! For example, the Gifted Adults Foundation in the Netherlands produced a leaflet on what it is like for a very high-IQ person to go to the doctor.[6] This highlighted that the consultation can go badly because doctors can find it unwelcome and unpleasant to deal with high-IQ patients' characteristic questioning, independent research, and reluctance to accept the doctor's authority.

A consultation with a very low-IQ patient can also be unpleasant for different reasons. Doctors might find it difficult to make themselves understood by the patient or relate to the patient's frame of reference. By understanding and being more prepared for how we react when we encounter difference, we can have more control over how the encounter goes.

CONCLUDING COMMENTS

If we would like it to, the "three ages" framework can become a tool in critically evaluating whatever we come across, towards choosing what we wish to do with it or about it. You might find it interesting to look at educationalists, policy-makers, and intelligence-field researchers and writers and consider in which age you would place their way of thinking, regardless of the historical timing of their work. (For example, I see Tiedemann as an Age of Integration thinker because of his attitudes and approach, even though his work took place in the 19th century and I have placed the Age of Integration as chronologically beginning in the 21st century.) At the end of this book under "Further Reading" I have named a few books which I have grouped into the ages that I see them as being most representative of.

My vision for an Age of Integration future is that people like Ida, Rita, and Carl could be better understood, and that intelligence could move from being a contentious and provocative topic that is almost forbidden to mention to being something that can be more openly faced and embraced. During my research interviews with very high-IQ individuals, many told me how strange and yet helpful it was to be able to talk about this paradoxically prominent yet hidden dimension of people's individual differences in intellectual functioning. Since my first book came out, I have received so many emails from readers for whom it has opened floodgates of emotions, memories, and sense-making. They have expressed the relief of having something important in their lives recognised and understood and of experiencing that it is suddenly possible to start exploring this previously taboo topic. As a psychotherapist, my professional practice is about not avoiding difficult conversations. Some notoriously difficult conversations are those that involve talking about money, sex, or politics. My invitation is: let's talk about intelligence!

This book has introduced a simplifying framework with which to view Western society's history, present, and envisaged future regarding the subject of human intelligence. It has explored the psychology underlying our approach to intelligence and emphasised that it is that psychology that needs to be tackled if we are to avoid simply repeating previous eras' problems. Moving on from the Age of Idealisation and also from the Age of Devaluation, I have argued for a "coming of age" in our approach to intelligence by embracing an Age of Integration. This would involve terminating discrimination in relation to human intelligence and creating an ethos in which all varieties of human beings and human brains are supported to function the best way they can, for the benefit of all. As each of us goes about our daily lives, we can notice signs around us of – and differences between – Age of Idealisation approaches, Age of Devaluation approaches, and Age of Integration approaches. And each of us can choose which approach we would like to take in how we react to and talk about, or ignore, human intelligence.

FURTHER READING

Throughout this book, publications are referred to that are listed in the reference list at the end, and these give plenty of further reading. However, I am listing here a few books, in chronological order, that I see as being representative of the perspectives of the different ages I have outlined and which demonstrate how strongly their perspectives contrast against each other. I stress that I *do not agree with* or recommend the perspectives of the books under the Age of Idealisation or the Age of Devaluation headings. I personally support an Age of Integration ethos, and so the books I have listed under that heading are ones that I do recommend.

AGE OF IDEALISATION

Galton, F. (1869). *Hereditary Genius: An Inquiry into Its Causes and Consequences*. London: Macmillan.

Goddard, H. H. (1912). *The Kallikak Family: A Study in the Heredity of Feeble-Mindedness*. New York: Macmillan.

AGE OF DEVALUATION

Kamin, L. (1974). *The Science and Politics of IQ*. New York: Routledge.

Gould, S. J. (1981). *The Mismeasure of Man*. New York: W. W. Norton & Company.

Stobart, G. (2014). *The Expert Learner: Challenging the Myth of Ability*. Berkshire, UK: Open University Press.

AGE OF INTEGRATION

Silberman, S. (2015). *Neurotribes*. Melbourne, MAM: Allen & Unwin.

Haier, R. J. (2017). *The Neuroscience of Intelligence*. Cambridge: Cambridge University Press.

Hambrick, D. Z., Campitelli, G. & Macnamara, B. N. (Eds.). (2018). *The Science of Expertise*. New York: Routledge.

Falck, S. (2020). *Extreme Intelligence: Development, Predicaments, Implications*. London: Routledge.

NOTES

EXPLAINING THE BOOK

1 See Warne et al. (2018).
2 Fichte (1794). (This is often incorrectly attributed to Hegel.)
3 Kuhn (1962).
4 Spearman (1904).
5 Gottfredson (1997: 13).
6 Cambridge University Press (2020).
7 Woodley of Menie et al. (2018); Warne et al. (2018).

CHAPTER 1

1 See Dweck (2000).
2 Aczel et al. (2015).
3 Lee et al. (2017).
4 Reynolds & Gifford (2001).
5 Murphy et al. (2003).
6 Lee et al. (2017).
7 Lee et al. (2017).
8 Murphy et al. (2003).
9 Murphy et al. (2003).
10 Boutwell et al. (2017).
11 Plomin & Deary (2015).

12 Webb et al. (2016: 24).

13 Towers (1987).

14 Judice & Neuberg (1998).

15 Spisak et al. (2014).

16 Simonton (1984).

17 Rosenberg et al. (2009); Hallgren et al. (2014).

18 Esslinger & Widner (2017: 5).

19 Esslinger & Widner (2017).

20 Hunt (2011); Ritchie (2015); Warne et al. (2018).

21 Sternberg (1985a).

22 Putnam & Killbride (1980).

23 Baral & Das (2004).

24 Yang & Sternberg (1997).

25 Wootton (2010).

26 Karpinski et al. (2018).

27 Herrnstein & Murray (1994).

CHAPTER 2

1 Sternberg (1990: 23).

2 Mitchell (2018).

3 Mackintosh (2011).

4 Cited in Ritchie (2015).

5 Webb (2014).

6 Webb (2014).

7 Neugebauer (1996).

8 Plucker & Esping (2014: 42).

9 Eyeoyibo (2018).

10 Cited in Sternberg (1990: 23).

11 Silverman (2013: 53).

12 Dweck (2000: 26).

13 Sykes (2008).

14 Webb (2014).

15 Plucker & Esping (2014).

16 Galton (1869).

17 Darwin (1859/2012).

18 Plucker & Esping (2014: 27).

19 Mackintosh (2011).

20 Plucker & Esping (2014).

21 Numerous publications. His first seminal book is Bowlby (1969).

22 For example, see Cassidy & Shaver (2008).

23 See Gomez (1997).

24 Tajfel & Turner (1979).

25 Cited in Brignell (2010).

26 Bashford & Levine (2010).

27 See Bashford & Levine (2010).

28 See the United States Holocaust Memorial Museum (n.d.).

CHAPTER 3

1 Woodley of Menie et al. (2018).

2 Gould (1981).

3 Mackintosh (2011: 17).

4 Hunt (2011).

5 Steele (1997).

6 Gordon & Rudert (1979).

7 Sternberg (1985b).

8 Sternberg (1997).

9 Sternberg (1999: 293).

10 Gardner (1983).

11 Gardner (1999).

12 Gardner (2004).

13 Horn & Cattell (1966).

14 Carroll (1993).

15 Mackintosh (2011).

16 Carroll (1866: 34).

17 Mahdawi (2017).

18 Kanazawa (2012).

19 A term coined by journalist Parry, R. (2006). Why capitol pages fear retaliation. *Consortium News.* www.consortiumnews.com/2006/100206.html. Cited in Woodley of Menie et al. (2018).

20 Woodley of Menie et al. (2018: 84).

21 A detailed list of such researchers can be found in Nyborg (2003).

22 Woodley of Menie et al. (2018).

23 Tucker (2009).

24 Woodley of Menie et al. (2018).

25 Woodley of Menie et al. (2018).

26 Griggs (2014).

27 Goleman (1996).

28 Waterhouse (2006).

29 Charlton (2009).

30 Ericsson et al. (1993).

31 See Falck (2020: 33).

32 Gladwell (2008).

33 Stobart (2014).

34 See back cover of Stobart (2014).

35 Davis (1978).

36 Pham (2007).

37 Kanazawa (2012: 1).

38 Cited in Silverman (2013: 51).

39 Smith (2018: 2).

40 Smith (2018: 11).

41 Feather (2012).

42 Coyle (2010).

43 Coyle (2010: 181).

44 American Psychiatric Association (2013).

45 See Haier (2017).

46 Kamin (1974).

47 Woodley of Menie et al. (2018: 85).

48 Gagné (2013).

49 *Intelligence* (2014).

50 Ruthsatz et al. (2014).

51 Ruthsatz & Detterman (2003).

52 Gagné (2013).

53 Cited in Simonton (2009).

CHAPTER 4

1 Blake (1994/1794).

2 Haier (2017).

3 Bakhiet et al. (2017).

4 See Haier (2017).

5 See Haier (2017).

6 See Haier (2017).

7 See Warne et al. (2018).

8 Hunter & Schmidt (2000: 151), cited in Warne et al. (2018: 44).

9 Maltby et al. (2017: 309).

10 Carroll (1993).

11 Ritchie (2015).

12 Cited in Warne et al. (2018: 41).

13 Cited in Warne et al. (2018: 41).

14 For example Haier (2017); Ritchie (2015); Hunt (2011).

15 See Mitchell (2018).

16 Ritchie (2015).

17 Haier (2017).

18 See Haier (2017).

19 A comprehensive review of these can be found in Haier (2017).

20 See Hunt (2011).

21 Hunt (2011). See also Protzko (2015).

22 See Falck (2020: 44).

23 See Haier (2017).

24 Bostrom (2014: 44).

25 Hunt (2011).

26 See Hunt (2011); Ritchie (2015); Haier (2017).

27 Hunt (2011).

28 See Hunt (2011).

29 Hunt (2011: 24).

30 See Warne et al. (2018).

31 Rindermann et al. (2020).

32 Cited in Warne et al. (2018: 38).

33 Karpinski et al. (2018).

34 In Reynolds & Willson (1985).

35 Schneider et al. (2014).

36 Deary et al. (2009).

37 Flynn (1984, 1987).

38 Kanazawa (2012).

39 Lynn (1998).

40 Meisenberg (2010).

41 See Haier (2017).

42 Crespi (2016).

43 Karpinski et al. (2018).

44 Equality Act (2010).

45 Hunt et al. (2018).

46 Falck (2020); Nauta & Ronner (2016); Corten et al. (2006).

47 Silverman (2013).

48 Mensa website (n.d.).

49 Caven (2019).

50 Silberman (2015: 3).

51 Winnicott (1963).

52 McAteer, D. (2010: 6).

53 Maslow (1943).

CHAPTER 5

1 Warne et al. (2018).

2 Gottfredson (2009).

3 Warne et al. (2018: 41).

4 Cited in Warne et al. (2018).

5 Warne et al. (2018).

6 QAA (2019).

7 Hunt (2014), cited in Warne et al. (2018).

8 APA (2014), cited in Warne et al. (2018).

9 This is a sample of my "Reflective Prompts", in Falck (2020).

10 Howell (2019).

11 Hunt (2011: 346).

12 See Goodwin & Gustavson (2012).

13 Stobart (2014: 19).

14 See Clynes (2016).

15 Cited in Warne et al. (2018).

16 Cited in Warne et al. (2018).

17 Kubiszewski (2014).

18 Karpinski et al. (2018).

19 Webb et al. (2016).

20 Smiley (2005).

21 Hemmings et al. (2018: 232).

22 Karpinski et al. (2018).

23 Gale et al. (2013).

24 Sugarman (2004: 40).

25 Moodley & Lubin (2008).

26 Cited in Warne et al. (2018).

27 Parkin et al. (2018).

28 Cited in Parkin et al. (2018).

29 Silverman (2013: 86).

30 Hirschi (1969).

31 Abagnale & Redding (1980).

IN CONCLUSION

1 Warne et al. (2018: 45).

2 Burhan et al. (2014).

3 See Kaufman (2009).

4 Dweck (2006).

5 Ingram & Morris (2007).

6 IHBV (2016).

REFERENCES

Abagnale, F. W. & Redding, S. (1980). *Catch Me If You Can*. Edinburgh: Mainstream Publishing Company.

Aczel, B., Palfi, B. & Kekecs, Z. (2015). What is stupid? People's conception of unintelligent behaviour. *Intelligence*, 53, pp. 51–58.

American Psychiatric Association. (2013). *Diagnostic and Statistical Manual of Mental Disorders: DSM-5* (5th ed.). Washington, DC: American Psychiatric Publishing.

Bakhiet, S. F. A., Essa, Y. A. S., Dwieb, A. M. M., Elsayed, A. M. A., Sulman, A. S. M., Cheng, H. & Lynn, R. (2017). Correlations between intelligence, head circumference and height: evidence from two samples in Saudi Arabia. *Journal of Biosocial Science*, 40(2), pp. 279–280.

Baral, B. & Das, J. P. (2004). Intelligence: what is indigenous to India and what is shared? In R. J. Sternberg (Ed.), *International Handbook of Intelligence* (pp. 270–301). Cambridge: Cambridge University Press.

Bashford, A. & Levine, P. (2010). *The Oxford Handbook of the History of Eugenics*. New York: Oxford University Press.

Blake, W. (1994/1794). *The Marriage of Heaven and Hell*. New York: Dover Publications.

Bostrom, N. (2014). *Superintelligence*. Oxford: Oxford University Press.

Boutwell, B. B., Meldrum, R. C. & Petkovsek, M. A. (2017). General intelligence in friendship selection: a study of preadolescent best friend dyads. *Intelligence*, 64, pp. 20–35.

Bowlby, J. (1969). *Attachment and Loss: Vol. 1, Attachment*. New York: Basic Books.

Brignell, V. (2010). British eugenics disabled. *The New Statesman* [online]. Available at: www.newstatesman.com/society/2010/12/british-eugenics-disabled [Accessed 16 October 2018].

Burhan, N. A. S., Mohamad, M. R., Kurniawan, Y. & Sidek, A. H. (2014). The impact of low, average, and high IQ on economic growth and technological progress: do all individuals contribute equally? *Intelligence*, 46, pp. 1–8.

Cambridge University Press. (2020). *Cambridge Advanced Learner's Dictionary & Thesaurus*. Cambridge: Cambridge University Press.

Carroll, J. B. (1993). *Human Cognitive Abilities*. Cambridge: Cambridge University Press.

Carroll, L. (1866). *Alice's Adventures in Wonderland*. London: Macmillan & Co.

Cassidy, J. & Shaver, P. R. (Eds.). (2008). *Handbook of Attachment: Theory, Research, and Clinical Applications* (2nd ed.). New York: The Guilford Press.

Caven, J. (2019). Bang up beasts who call us geeks! Cry-baby nerds want jokers sent to jail. *Daily Star*, front page, 18 December.

Charlton, B. G. (2009). Clever sillies: why high IQ people tend to be deficient in common sense. *Medical Hypotheses*, 73(6), pp. 867–870.

Clynes, T. (2016). How to raise a genius. *Nature*, 537, pp. 152–155.

Corten, F., Nauta, N. & Ronner, S. (2006). *Highly Intelligent and Gifted Employees – Key to Innovation?* (English translation). Academic paper delivered in Amsterdam, 11 October 2006 at International HRD-Conference [online]. Available at: www.triplenine.org/articles/Nauta-200610.pdf [Accessed 12 June 2012].

Coyle, D. (2010). *The Talent Code: Greatness Isn't Born. It's Grown*. London: Arrow Books.

Crespi, B. J. (2016). Autism as a disorder of high intelligence. *Frontiers in Neuroscience*, 10. doi:10.3389/fnins.2016.00300.

Darwin, C. (1859/2012). *On the Origin of Species by Means of Natural Selection*. London: Arcturus Publishing Ltd.

Davis, B. (1978). The moralistic fallacy. *Nature*, 272, p. 390.

Deary, I. J., Corley, J., Gow, A. J., Harris, S. E., Houlihan, L. M., Marioni, R. E., Penke, L., Rafnsson, S. B. & Starr, J. M. (2009). Age-associated cognitive decline. *British Medical Bulletin*, 92(1), pp. 135–152.

Dweck, C. S. (2000). *Self-Theories*. Philadelphia: Psychology Press.

Dweck, C. S. (2006). *Mindset: How You Can Fulfil Your Potential*. London: Constable & Robinson Ltd.

Equality Act. (2010). [online]. Available at: www.legislation.gov.uk/ukpga/2010/15/contents [Accessed 26 February 2020].

Ericsson, K. A., Krampe, R. T. & Tesch-Romer, C. (1993). The role of deliberate practice in the acquisition of expert performance. *Psychological Review*, 100, pp. 364–403.

Esslinger, M. & Widner, D. (2017). *Escaping Alcatraz*. San Francisco: Ocean View Publishing.

Eyeoyibo, M. (2018). The mental health of people with intellectual disabilities. In C. Hemmings (Ed.), *Mental Health in Intellectual Disabilities* (5th ed., pp. 1–7). Hove: Pavilion Publishing and Media Ltd.

Falck, S. (2020). *Extreme Intelligence: Development, Predicaments, Implications*. London: Routledge.

Feather, N. (2012). Tall poppies, deservingness and schadenfreude. *The Psychologist*, 25(6), pp. 434–437.

Fichte, J. (1794). Review of *Aenesidemus*. Reprinted in Breazeale, D. (Ed. and Trans.). (1988). *Fichte: Early Philosophical Writings*. New York: Cornell University Press.

Flynn, J. R. (1984). The mean IQ of Americans: massive gains 1932 to 1978. *Psychological Bulletin*, 95, pp. 29–51.

Flynn, J. R. (1987). Massive IQ gains in 14 nations: what IQ tests really measure. *Psychological Bulletin*, 101, pp. 171–191.

Gagné, F. (2013). Yes, giftedness (aka "innate" talent) does exist! In S. B. Kaufman (Ed.), *The Complexity of Greatness* (pp. 191–221). Oxford: Oxford University Press.

Gale, C. R., Batty, G. D., McIntosh, A. M., Porteous, D. J., Deary, I. J. & Rasmussen, F. (2013). Is bipolar disorder more common in highly intelligent people? A cohort study of a million men. *Molecular Psychiatry*, 18(2), pp. 190–194.

Galton, F. (1869). *Hereditary Genius: An Inquiry into Its Causes and Consequences*. London: Macmillan.

Gardner, H. (1983). *Frames of Mind: The Theory of Multiple Intelligences*. New York: Basic Books.

Gardner, H. (1999). *Intelligence Reframed*. New York: Basic Books.

Gardner, H. (2004). Audiences for the theory of multiple intelligences. *Teachers College Record*, 106, pp. 212–220.

Gladwell, M. (2008). *Outliers: The Story of Success*. London: Allen Lane.

Goleman, D. (1996). *Emotional Intelligence: Why It Can Matter More Than IQ*. London: Bloomsbury.

Gomez, L. (1997). *An Introduction to Object Relations*. London: Free Association Books.

Goodwin, C. B. & Gustavson, M. (2012). Education outside of the box: home-schooling your gifted or twice-exceptional child. *Understanding Our Gifted*, 24(4), pp. 8–11.

Gordon, R. A. & Rudert, E. E. (1979). Bad news concerning IQ tests. *Sociology of Education*, 52(3), pp. 174–190.

Gottfredson, L. S. (1997). Mainstream science on intelligence: an editorial with 52 signatories, history and bibliography. *Intelligence*, 24, pp. 13–23.

Gottfredson, L. S. (2009). Logical fallacies used to dismiss the evidence on intelligence testing. In R. P. Phelps (Ed.), *Correcting Fallacies About Educational and Psychological Testing* (pp. 11–65). Washington, DC: American Psychological Association.

Gould, S. J. (1981). *The Mismeasure of Man*. New York: W. W. Norton & Company.

Griggs, R. A. (2014). Topical coverage in introductory textbooks from the 1980s through the 2000s. *Teaching of Psychology*, 41, pp. 5–10.

Haier, R. J. (2017). *The Neuroscience of Intelligence*. Cambridge: Cambridge University Press.

Hallgren, M., Nygard, L. & Kottorp, A. (2014). Everyday technology use among people with mental retardation: relevance, perceived difficulty, and influencing factors. *Scandinavian Journal of Occupational Therapy*, 21(3), pp. 210–218.

Hemmings, J., Jain, D. & Htut, S. (2018). Key facts, concepts and principles in the mental health of people with intellectual disabilities. In C. Hemmings (Ed.), *Mental Health in Intellectual Disabilities* (5th ed., pp. 231–244). Hove: Pavilion Publishing and Media Ltd.

Herrnstein, R. J. & Murray, C. (1994). *The Bell Curve: Intelligence and Class Structure in American Life*. New York: Free Press.

Hirschi, T. (1969). *Causes of Delinquency*. Berkeley, CA: University of California Press.

Horn, J. L. & Cattell, R. B. (1966). Refinement and test of the theory of fluid and crystallised general intelligences. *Journal of Educational Psychology*, 57(5), pp. 253–270.

Howell, R. (2019). *Book Launch* [email]. Personal correspondence, 25 November.

Hunt, E. (2011). *Human Intelligence*. New York: Cambridge University Press.

Hunt, V., Prince, S., Dixon-Fyle, S. & Yee, L. (2018). *Delivering Through Diversity*. McKinsey & Company [online]. Available at: www.mckinsey.com/~/media/McKinsey/Business%20Functions/Organization/Our%20Insights/Delivering%20through%20diversity/Delivering-through-diversity_full-report.ashx [Accessed 26 February 2020].

IHBV. (2016). *A Gifted Person Goes to the Doctor* . . . Amersfoort: Gifted Adults Foundation [online]. Available at: https://ihbv.nl/wp-content/uploads/2014/08/IBHV-leaflet_A-gifted-person-goes-to-the-doctor.pdf [Accessed 5 April 2020].

Ingram, P. & Morris, M. W. (2007). Do people mix at mixers? Structure, homophily, and the 'life of the party'. *Administrative Science Quarterly*, 52(4), pp. 558–585.

Intelligence. (2014). Special volume: acquiring expertise. Ability, practice, and other influences. *Intelligence*, 45, pp. 1–124, July–August.

Judice, T. N. & Neuberg, S. L. (1998). When interviewers desire to confirm negative expectations: self-fulfilling prophecies and inflated applicant self-perceptions. *Basic and Applied Social Psychology*, 20(3), pp. 175–190.

Kamin, L. (1974). *The Science and Politics of IQ*. New York: Routledge.

Kanazawa, S. (2012). *The Intelligence Paradox*. Hoboken, NJ: John Wiley & Sons.

Karpinski, R. I., Kinase Kolb, A. M., Tetreault, N. A. & Borowski, T. B. (2018). High intelligence: a risk factor for psychological and physiological overexcitabilities. *Intelligence*, 66, pp. 8–23.

Kaufman, A. S. (2009). *IQ Testing 101*. New York: Springer Publishing Company.

Kubiszewski, I. (2014). Beyond GDP: are there better ways to measure well-being? *The Conversation* [online]. Available at: https://theconversation.com/beyond-gdp-are-there-better-ways-to-measure-well-being-33414 [Accessed 5 April 2020].

Kuhn, T. (1962). *The Structure of Scientific Revolutions*. Chicago: University of Chicago Press.

Lee, A. J., Hibbs, C., Wright, M. J., Martin, N. G., Keller, M. C. & Zietsch, B. P. (2017). Assessing the accuracy of perceptions of intelligence based on heritable facial features. *Intelligence*, 64, pp. 1–8.

Lynn, R. (1998). In support of the nutrition theory. In U. Neisser (Ed.), *The Rising Curve: Long-Term Gains in IQ and Related Measures* (pp. 207–215). Washington, DC: American Psychological Association.

Mackintosh, N. J. (2011). *IQ and Human Intelligence* (2nd ed.). Oxford: Oxford University Press.

Mahdawi, A. (2017). Having a high IQ is a curse . . . just look at Donald Trump. *The Guardian*, 10 December [online]. Available at: www.theguardian.com/science/2017/dec/10/having-a-high-iq-is-a-curse-just-look-at-donald-trump [Accessed 1 April 2020].

Maltby, J., Day, L. & Macaskill, A. (2017). *Personality, Individual Differences and Intelligence* (4th ed.). Harlow: Pearson.

Maslow, A. H. (1943). A theory of human motivation. *Psychological Review*, 50(4), pp. 370–396.

McAteer, D. (2010). Philosophical pluralism: navigating the sea of diversity in psychotherapeutic and counselling psychology practice. In M. Milton (Ed.), *Therapy and Beyond: Counselling Psychology Contributions to Therapeutic and Social Issues* (pp. 5–20). Chichester: Wiley-Blackwell.

Meisenberg, G. (2010). The reproduction of intelligence. *Intelligence*, 38, pp. 220–230.

Mensa Website. (n.d.). *Bright Children Bullied for "Being Different"* [online]. Available at: www. mensa.org.uk/news/bright-children-bullied-being-different [Accessed 8 March 2020].

Mitchell, P. W. (2018). The fault in his seeds: lost notes to the case of bias in Samuel George Morton's cranial race science. *PLOS Biology*. doi:10.1371/journal.pbio.2007008.

Moodley, R. & Lubin, D. B. (2008). Developing your career to working with multicultural and diversity clients. In S. Palmer & R. Bor (Eds.), *The Practitioner's Handbook: A Guide for Counsellors, Psychotherapists and Counselling Psychologists* (pp. 156–157). London: Sage.

Murphy, N. A., Hall, J. A. & Colvin, C. R. (2003). Accurate intelligence assessments in social interactions: mediators and gender effects. *Journal of Personality*, 71(3), pp. 465–493.

Nauta, N. & Ronner, S. (2016). *Gifted Workers, Hitting the Target*. Utrecht: Big Business Publishers.

Neugebauer, R. (1996). Mental handicap in medieval and early modern England. In D. Wright & A. Digby (Eds.), *From Idiocy to Mental Deficiency*. London: Routledge.

Nyborg, H. (2003). The sociology of psychometric and bio-behavioral sciences: a case study of destructive social reductionism and collective fraud in 20th century academia. In H. Nyborg (Ed.), *The Scientific Study of General Intelligence: Tribute to Arthur R. Jensen* (pp. 441–502). New York: Pergamon.

Parkin, E., Kennedy, S., Bate, A., Long, R., Hubble, S. & Powell, A. (2018). *Learning Disability – Policy and Services*. Briefing Paper, Number 07058. London: House of Commons Library.

Pham, M. T. (2007). Emotion and rationality: a critical review and interpretation of empirical evidence. *Review of General Psychology*. doi:10.1037/1089-2680.11.2.155.

Plomin, R. & Deary, I. J. (2015). Genetics and intelligence differences: five special findings. *Molecular Psychiatry*, 20, pp. 98–108.

Plucker, J. A. & Esping, A. (2014). *Intelligence 101*. New York: Springer Publishing Company.

Protzko, J. (2015). The environment in raising early intelligence: a meta-analysis of the fadeout effect. *Intelligence*, 53, pp. 202–210.

Putnam, D. B. & Killbride, P. L. (1980). *A Relativistic Understanding of Social Intelligence Among the Songhay of Mali and Smaia of Kenya*. Presented at Meeting for Social and Cross-Cultural Research, Philadelphia, PA.

QAA. (2019). *Subject Benchmark Statement: Psychology* (5th ed.) [online]. Available at: www.qaa.ac.uk/docs/qaa/subject-benchmark-statements/subject-bench mark-statement-psychology.pdf?sfvrsn=6935c881_13 [Accessed 1 April 2020].

Reynolds, C. R. & Willson, V. L. (Eds.). (1985). *Methodological and Statistical Advances in the Study of Individual Differences*. New York: Plenum Press.

Reynolds, D. J. & Gifford, R. (2001). The sounds and sights of intelligence: a lens model channel analysis. *Personality and Social Psychology Bulletin*, 27(2), pp. 187–200.

Rindermann, H., Becker, D. & Coyle, T. R. (2020). Survey of expert opinion on intelligence: intelligence research, experts' background, controversial issues, and the media. *Intelligence*, 78, pp. 1–18.

Ritchie, S. J. (2015). *Intelligence: All That Matters*. London: John Murray Learning.

Rosenberg, L., Kottorp, A., Winblad, B. & Nygard, L. (2009). Perceived difficulty in everyday technology use among older adults with or without cognitive deficits. *Scandinavian Journal of Occupational Therapy*, 16(4), pp. 216–226.

Ruthsatz, J. & Detterman, D. K. (2003). An extraordinary memory: the case study of a musical prodigy. *Intelligence*, 31, pp. 509–518.

Ruthsatz, J., Ruthsatz, K. & Ruthsatz Stephens, K. (2014). Putting practice into perspective: child prodigies as evidence of innate talent. *Intelligence*, 45, pp. 60–65.

Schneider, W., Niklas, F. & Schmiedeler, S. (2014). Intellectual development from early childhood to early adulthood: the impact of early IQ differences on stability and change over time. *Learning and Individual Differences*, 32, pp. 156–162.

Silberman, S. (2015). *Neurotribes*. Melbourne, MAM: Allen & Unwin.

Silverman, L. K. (2013). *Giftedness 101*. New York: Springer Publishing Company.

Simonton, D. K. (1984). *Genius, Creativity, and Leadership: Historiometric Inquiries*. London: Harvard University Press.

Simonton, D. K. (2009). *Genius 101*. New York: Springer.

Smiley, E. (2005). Epidemiology of mental health problems in adults with learning disability: an update. *Advances in Psychiatric Treatment*, 11(3), pp. 214–222.

Smith, T. W. (2018). *Schadenfreude: The Joy of Another's Misfortune*. London: Profile Books Ltd.

Spearman, C. (1904). 'General intelligence', objectively determined and measured. *American Journal of Psychology*, 15, pp. 201–292.

Spisak, B. R., Blaker, N. M., Lefevre, C. E., Moore, F. R. & Krebbers, K. F. B. (2014). A face for all seasons: searching for context-specific leadership traits and discovering a general preference for perceived health. *Frontiers in Human Neuroscience*, 8. doi:10.3389/fnhum.2014.00792.

Steele, C. M. (1997). A threat in the air: how stereotypes shape intellectual identity and performance. *American Psychologist*, 52(6), pp. 613–629.

Sternberg, R. J. (1985a). Implicit theories of intelligence, creativity, and wisdom. *Journal of Personality and Social Psychology*, 49, pp. 607–627.

Sternberg, R. J. (1985b). *Beyond IQ: A Triarchic Theory of Human Intelligence*. New York: Cambridge University Press.

Sternberg, R. J. (1990). *Metaphors of Mind: Conceptions of the Nature of Intelligence*. New York: Cambridge University Press.

Sternberg, R. J. (1997). *Successful Intelligence*. New York: Plume.

Sternberg, R. J. (1999). The theory of successful intelligence. *Review of General Psychology*, 3, pp. 292–316.

Stobart, G. (2014). *The Expert Learner: Challenging the Myth of Ability*. Berkshire, UK: Open University Press.

Sugarman, L. (2004). *Counselling and the Life Course*. Los Angeles: Sage.

Sykes, T. (2008). My life on drugs at Eton College. *Telegraph* [online]. Available at: www.telegraph.co.uk/news/uknews/2695715/My-life-on-drugs-at-Eton-College.html [Accessed 1 March 2020].

Tajfel, H. & Turner, J. C. (1979). An integrative theory of intergroup conflict. Reprinted in Hatch, M. J. & Schultz, M. (Eds.). (2004). *Organizational Identity: A Reader* (pp. 56–65). Oxford: Oxford University Press.

Towers, G. M. (1987). The outsiders. *Gift of Fire*, 22 [online]. Available at: www.cpsimoes.net/artigos/outsiders.html. [Accessed 5 February 2017].

Tucker, W. H. (2009). *The Cattell Controversy: Race, Science, and Ideology*. Urbana, IL: University of Illinois Press.

United States Holocaust Memorial Museum. (n.d.). *Holocaust Encyclopedia* [online]. Available at: https://encyclopedia.ushmm.org/content/en/article/doc umenting-numbers-of-victims-of-the-holocaust-and-nazi-persecution [Accessed 1 March 2020].

Warne, R. T., Astle, M. C. & Hill, J. C. (2018). What do undergraduates learn about human intelligence? An analysis of introductory psychology textbooks. *Archives of Scientific Psychology*, 6, pp. 32–50.

Waterhouse, L. (2006). Multiple intelligences, the Mozart effect, and emotional intelligence: a critical review. *Educational Psychologist*, 41(4), pp. 207–225.

Webb, J. T. (2014). *A Guide to Psychological Understanding of People with Learning Disabilities*. Hove: Routledge.

Webb, J. T., Amend, E. R., Beljan, P., Webb, N. E., Kuzujanakis, M., Olenchak, F. R. & Goerss, J. (2016). *Misdiagnosis and Dual Diagnoses of Gifted Children and Adults* (2nd ed.). Tucson, AZ: Great Potential Press.

Winnicott, D. W. (1963). The development of the capacity for concern. Reprinted in Winnicott, D. W. (Ed.). (2018). *The Maturational Processes and the Facilitating Environment*. London: Routledge.

Woodley of Menie, M. A., Dutton, E., Figueredo, A-J., Carl, N., Debes, F., Hertler, S., Irwing, P., Kura, K., Lynn, R., Madison, G., Meisenber, G., Miller, E. M., te Nijenhuis, J., Nyborg, H. & Rindermann, H. (2018). Communicating intelligence research: media misrepresentation, the Gould effect, and unexpected forces. *Intelligence*, 70, pp. 84–87.

Wootton, D. (2010). *Galileo: Watcher of the Skies*. New Haven: Yale University Press.

Yang, S. & Sternberg, R. J. (1997). Conceptions of intelligence in ancient Chinese philosophy. *Journal of Theoretical and Philosophical Psychology*, 17, pp. 101–119.